THE FOLGER LIBRARY SHAKESPEARE

Designed to make Shakespeare's classic plays available to the general reader, each edition contains a reliable text with modernized spelling and punctuation, scene-by-scene plot summaries, and explanatory notes clarifying obscure and obsolete expressions. An interpretive essay and accounts of Shakespeare's life and theater form an instructive preface to each play.

Louis B. Wright, General Editor, was the Director of the Folger Shakespeare Library from 1948 until his retirement in 1968. He is the author of *Middle-Class Culture in Elizabethan England, Religion and Empire, Shakespeare for Everyman,* and many other books and essays on the history and literature of the Tudor and Stuart periods.

Virginia Lamar, Assistant Editor, served as research assistant to the Director and Executive Secretary of the Folger Shakespeare Library from 1946 until her death in 1968. She is the author of *English Dress in the Age of Shakespeare* and *Travel and Roads in England,* and coeditor of William Strachey's *Historie of Travell into Virginia Britania.*

The Folger Shakespeare Library

GENERAL EDITOR

LOUIS B. WRIGHT

Director, Folger Shakespeare Library, 1948–1968

ASSISTANT EDITOR

VIRGINIA A. LaMAR

Executive Secretary, Folger Shakespeare Library, 1946–1968

THE COMEDY
OF ERRORS

By

WILLIAM
SHAKESPEARE

PUBLISHED BY POCKET BOOKS NEW YORK

POCKET BOOKS, a Simon & Schuster division of
GULF & WESTERN CORPORATION
1230 Avenue of the Americas, New York, N.Y. 10020

ISBN: 0-671-48809-0

First Pocket Books printing February, 1964

7th printing

Trademarks registered in the United States and other countries.

Printed in the U.S.A.

Preface

This edition of *The Comedy of Errors* is designed to make available a readable text of one of Shakespeare's early comedies. In the centuries since Shakespeare, many changes have occurred in the meanings of words, and some clarification of Shakespeare's vocabulary may be helpful. To provide the reader with necessary notes in the most accessible format, we have placed them on the pages facing the text that they explain. We have tried to make these notes as brief and simple as possible. Preliminary to the text we have also included a brief statement of essential information about Shakespeare and his stage. Readers desiring more detailed information should refer to the books suggested in the references, and if still further information is needed, the bibliographies in those books will provide the necessary clues to the literature of the subject.

The early texts of Shakespeare's plays provide only scattered stage directions and no indications of setting, and it is conventional for modern editors to add these to clarify the action. Such additions, and additions to entrances and exits, as well as many indications of act and scene division, are placed in square brackets.

All illustrations are from material in the Folger Library collections.

L. B. W.

V. A. L.

May 21, 1963

Apprentice Work in Farce

If Shakespeare had been a schoolmaster in the country before going up to London to make his fortune in the theatre—as one biographer thought he might have been—he could have chosen no more schoolmasterish play for his first endeavor in comedy than *The Comedy of Errors*. This play follows more closely the tradition of Roman comedy than any other drama attributed to Shakespeare, and is one of his earliest efforts in writing for the stage, perhaps the very earliest comedy from his pen. It was precisely the kind of play that would have appealed to a young man whose grammar school memories of Plautus and Terence were still fresh, the kind of play that schoolboys sometimes performed.

The Comedy of Errors probably dates from sometime between 1592 and 1594. A clear reference occurs in an account of a performance at Gray's Inn on December 28, 1594, when this play was part of a riotous celebration by the young lawyers of the Inn. Allusions to the French civil war between 1589 and 1593, when Henry of Navarre was trying to establish his right to the French crown, suggest a date of composition before the settlement of the French dispute by the truce of July, 1593. Though the precise date and place of first performance are uncertain, it is early enough for us to be sure that *The Comedy of Errors* is apprentice work of its author.

Although *The Comedy of Errors* is not a slavish imitation of Plautus, it follows very closely the plot outline of his *Menaechmi*. The scene in which the husband is locked out of his own house may have been suggested by a similar situation in Plautus' *Amphitruo*. To complicate the plot even more than in Plautus' *Menaechmi*, Shakespeare added a pair of servants who were twins. He also introduced the Abbess, who delivered a sermon to Adriana on the consequences of a jealous wife's railings, a passage delivered with such fervent sincerity that some critics have thought that it reflects Shakespeare's unhappy experience with Anne Hathaway. Sir Edmund Chambers, in discounting this view, comments: "Poor Anne Hathaway, of whom after all we know nothing but that she had a honeysuckle name, and was some years older than Shakespeare, and was kind to him before marriage, and received a legacy of his second-best bed." The jealous wife was so common a convention in Elizabethan literature that no biographical significance need attach to the theme. Indeed, with the exception of the Abbess' lecture, Adriana's jealousy is largely expressed in her own speeches, which are too laden with genuine

MENAECMI.

¶ A pleasant and fine Con-
ceited Comœdie, taken out of the most excellent wittie Poet *Plautus*:

*Chosen purposely from out the rest, as least harmefull, and
yet most delightfull.*

Written in English, by *VV. VV.*

LONDON
Printed by Tho. Creede,
and are to be sold by William Barley, at his
shop in Gratious streete.

1595.

The title page of William Warner's translation of Plautus'
Menaechmi (1595).

distress to be comic. If Shakespeare was inspired by a personal marital experience, he did not make the most of an opportunity to champion husbands against the jealousy of their wives.

Since the main source of the play is Plautus' *Menaechmi*, scholars have wondered whether Shakespeare's Latin was sufficient for him to have read the original. It probably was. But he could easily have had the plot related to him by any one of a host of good Latinists who were familiar with the play. Both Plautus and Terence were known to most grammar school students. It has been argued that Shakespeare may have had an older adaptation of Plautus in English to work from, but, if he had, all records of such an original play in English have disappeared. William Warner published a translation of the *Menaechmi* in 1595, and it is possible that Shakespeare could have seen the translation in manuscript, which, the preface indicates, circulated "for the use and delight of his [the translator's] private friends." The most reasonable view of Shakespeare's use of the source play is that he read the *Menaechmi* in the Latin.

On the stage, *The Comedy of Errors* has proved an effective piece of entertainment, whatever one may think of it as drama. It cannot be called a notable contribution to English comedy, and it is a far cry indeed from Shakespeare's own great comedies. It is essentially a farce, with a fair amount of slapstick buffoonery as the plot of mistaken identity unfolds and the two Dromios receive the beatings that were characteristic of Roman comedy. The dialogue is full of wordplay that was a convention of both Roman comedy and tragedy. Such wordplay was also a favorite device of Elizabethan drama, particularly in the 1590's.

Literal-minded playgoers will find the mistaken identity theme totally absurd and so unrealistic as to make the play unbelievable. But many dramas require the spectator to grant the illusion of possibility before they can be relished. In the theatre one must surrender one's notions of actuality and accept the conventions of the piece, whatever it is, and then enjoy the working-out of the plot. If one should insist upon a criterion of reasonableness, most operas would be unacceptable. The acceptance of a set of absurd situations is essential in farce, and that is what Shakespeare requires of the spectator in *The Comedy of Errors*. With reasonably competent actors, audiences find such acceptance easy, and *The Comedy of Errors* has provided amusement from Shakespeare's time until now.

Farce has had a long history as entertainment, dating from the classical world and lasting until our time, and slapstick has probably provided amusement in the theatre since theatres have existed. Although Shakespeare's indebtedness to Roman drama is obvious in his adaptation from Plautus, he had behind him a native tradition of farce which gave to the buffoonery of *The Comedy of Errors* a familiarity that added to its theatrical effectiveness. Even the mystery and morality plays had consistently inserted farcical scenes for the delectation of their audiences. Noah and his wife in the Wakefield Shipwrights' play had engaged in a boisterous quarrel and fight; Mak, the rascally shepherd in the same cycle, gets himself tossed in a blanket. Herod traditionally roared, ranted, and pretended to capture small boys in the audience. The devils and the vices beat each other in comic encounters much like those still employed by circus clowns. For much of their comic entertainment, native plays before Shakespeare's time depended upon farcical situations that were as old as the human race. Consequently, Shakespeare's audience was already conditioned to farce and was ready to enjoy a play with the situations that *The Comedy of Errors* furnished.

Although we are not certain for what occasion Shakespeare wrote *The Comedy of Errors,* we do know that it provided acceptable entertainment at court as late as 1604, and it may have been presented at court on earlier occasions. Some allusions suggest that it may have been presented before Queen Elizabeth at Greenwich on December 28, 1594, preceding its performance at Gray's Inn for the reveling lawyers. The records show no revival during the Restoration, and there is no documentary evidence of performances again until Charles Macklin's production at Drury Lane in 1741. The play appeared at intervals during the second half of the eighteenth century and was revived frequently in the nineteenth century, often in altered versions.

Although this is the shortest of Shakespeare's plays, most alterations made it even briefer.

Frederic Reynolds produced at Covent Garden in 1819 a musical version of *The Comedy of Errors* which was a hodgepodge of songs from other Shakespearean plays. Shakespeare's play was also used as a point of departure for a free adaptation called *The Boys from Syracuse,* a musical production that proved popular on the American stage in 1938-39. A revival in 1963 proved a smash hit.

Although varied adaptations have kept the play alive over the centuries, Shakespeare's own version has not been unknown on the stage. In 1855, Samuel Phelps revived an unaltered version at Sadler's Wells in London, and since that time numerous performances of the play have kept it before the public. In 1963, productions of the play were scheduled by two of the leading Shakespearean companies on the North American continent. On the stage it proves amusing and acts far better than one would suspect. Like many of Shakespeare's other plays, it shows that the dramatist had a keen sense of the theatre very early in his career.

The only text is that of the First Folio, for *The Comedy of Errors* had no known quarto printing. The Folio version is reasonably free of errors but it shows some evidence of cutting. Since it is Shakespeare's shortest play, running to only 1,777 lines, a few critics have maintained that it survives in a version cut for production on tour, but this view is not generally accepted. One or two passages appear to have been garbled in printing and are difficult to explain.

THE AUTHOR

As early as 1598 Shakespeare was so well known as a literary and dramatic craftsman that Francis Meres, in his *Palladis Tamia: Wits Treasury*, referred in flattering terms to him as "mellifluous and honey-tongued Shakespeare," famous for his *Venus and Adonis*, his *Lucrece*, and "his sugared sonnets," which were circulating "among his private friends." Meres observes further that "as Plautus and Seneca are accounted the best for comedy and tragedy among the Latins, so Shakespeare among the English is the most excellent in both kinds for the stage," and he mentions a dozen plays that had made a name for Shakespeare. He concludes with the remark that "the Muses would speak with Shakespeare's fine filed phrase if they would speak English."

To those acquainted with the history of the Elizabethan and Jacobean periods, it is incredible that anyone should be so naïve or ignorant as to doubt the reality of Shakespeare as the author of the plays that bear his name. Yet so much nonsense has been written about other "candidates" for the plays that it is well to remind readers that no credible evidence that would stand up in a court of law has ever been adduced to prove either that Shakespeare did not write his plays or that anyone else wrote them. All the theories offered for the authorship of Francis Bacon, the Earl of Derby, the Earl of Oxford, the Earl of Hertford, Christopher Marlowe, and a score of other candidates are mere conjectures spun from the active imaginations of persons who confuse hypothesis and conjecture with evidence.

As Meres's statement of 1598 indicates, Shakespeare was already a popular playwright whose name carried weight at the box office. The obvious reputation of Shakespeare as early as 1598 makes the effort to prove him a myth one of the most absurd in the history of human perversity.

The anti-Shakespeareans talk darkly about a plot of vested interests to maintain the authorship of Shakespeare. Nobody has any vested interest in Shakespeare, but every scholar is interested in the truth and in the quality of evidence advanced by special pleaders who set forth hypotheses in place of facts.

The anti-Shakespeareans base their arguments upon a few simple premises, all of them false. These false premises are that Shakespeare was an unlettered yokel without any schooling, that nothing is known about Shakespeare, and that only a noble lord or the equivalent in background could have written the plays. The facts are that more is known about Shakespeare than about most dramatists of his day, that he had a very good education, acquired in the Stratford Grammar School, that the plays show no evidence of profound book learning, and that the knowledge of kings and courts evident in the plays is no greater than any intelligent young man could have picked up at second hand. Most anti-Shakespeareans are naïve and betray an obvious snobbery. The author of their favorite plays, they imply, must have had a college diploma framed and hung on his study wall like the one in their dentist's office, and obviously so great a writer must have had a title or some equally significant evidence of exalted social background. They forget that genius has a way of cropping up in unexpected places and that none of the great creative writers of the world got his inspiration in a college or university course.

William Shakespeare was the son of John Shakespeare of Stratford-upon-Avon, a substantial citizen of that small but busy market town in the center of the rich agricultural county of Warwick. John Shakespeare kept a shop, what we would call a general store; he dealt in wool and other produce and gradually acquired property. As a youth, John Shakespeare had learned the trade of glover and leather worker. There is no contemporary evidence that the elder Shakespeare was a butcher, though the anti-Shakespeareans like to talk about the ignorant "butcher's boy of Stratford." Their only evidence is a statement by gossipy John Aubrey, more than a century after William Shakespeare's birth, that young William followed his father's trade, and when he killed a calf, "he would do it in a high style and make a speech." We would like to believe the story true, but Aubrey is not a very credible witness.

John Shakespeare probably continued to operate a farm at Snitterfield that his father had leased. He married Mary Arden, daughter of his father's landlord, a man of some property. The third of their eight children was William, baptized on April 26, 1564, and probably born three days before. At least, it is conventional to celebrate April 23 as his birthday.

The Stratford records give considerable information about John Shakespeare. We know that he held several municipal offices including those of alderman and mayor. In 1580 he was in some sort of legal difficulty and was fined for neglecting a summons of the Court of Queen's Bench requiring him to appear at Westminster and be bound over to keep the peace.

As a citizen and alderman of Stratford, John Shakespeare was entitled to send his son to the grammar school free. Though the records are lost, there can be no reason to doubt that this is where young William received his education. As any student of the period knows, the grammar schools provided the basic education in Latin learning and literature. The Elizabethan grammar school is not to be confused with modern grammar schools. Many cultivated men of the day received all their formal education in the grammar schools. At the universities in this period a student would have received little training that would have inspired him to be a creative writer. At Stratford young Shakespeare would have acquired a familiarity with Latin and some little knowledge of Greek. He would have read Latin authors and become acquainted with the plays of Plautus and Terence. Undoubtedly, in this period of his life he received that stimulation to read and explore for himself the world of ancient and modern history which he later utilized in his plays. The youngster who does not acquire this type of intellectual curiosity *before* college days rarely develops as a result of a college course the kind of mind Shakespeare demonstrated. His learning in books was anything but profound, but he clearly had the probing curiosity that sent him in search of information, and he had a keenness in the observation of nature and of humankind that finds reflection in his poetry.

There is little documentation for Shakespeare's boyhood. There is little reason why there should be. Nobody knew that he was going to be a dramatist about whom any scrap of information would be prized in the centuries to come. He was merely an active and vigorous youth of Stratford, perhaps assisting his father in his business, and no Boswell bothered to write down facts about him. The most important record that we have is a marriage license issued by the Bishop of Worcester on November 27, 1582, to permit William Shakespeare to marry Anne Hathaway, seven or eight years his senior; furthermore, the Bishop permitted the marriage after reading the banns only once instead of three times, evidence of the desire for haste. The need was explained on May 26, 1583, when the christening of Susanna, daughter of William and Anne Shakespeare, was recorded at Stratford. Two years later, on February 2, 1585, the records show the birth of twins to the Shakespeares, a boy and a girl who were christened Hamnet and Judith.

What William Shakespeare was doing in Stratford during the early years of his married life, or when he went to London, we do not know. It has been conjectured that he tried his hand at school-teaching, but that is a mere guess. There is a legend that he left Stratford to escape a charge of poaching in the park of Sir Thomas Lucy of Charlecote, but there is no proof of this. There is also a legend that when first he came to London he earned his living by holding horses outside a playhouse and presently was given employment inside, but there is nothing better than eighteenth-century hearsay for this. How Shakespeare broke into the London theatres as a dramatist and actor we do not know. But lack of information is not surprising, for Elizabethans did not write their autobiographies, and we know even less about the lives of many writers and some men of affairs than we know about Shakespeare. By 1592 he was so well established and popular that he incurred the envy of the dramatist and pamphleteer Robert Greene, who referred to him as an "upstart crow . . . in his own conceit the only Shake-scene in a country." From this time onward, contemporary allusions and references in legal documents enable the scholar to chart Shakespeare's career with greater accuracy than is possible with most other Elizabethan dramatists.

By 1594 Shakespeare was a member of the company of actors known as the Lord Chamberlain's Men. After the accession of James I, in 1603, the company would have the sovereign for their patron and would be known as the King's Men. During the period of its greatest prosperity, this company would have as its principal theatres the Globe and the Blackfriars. Shakespeare was both an actor and a shareholder in the company. Tradition has assigned him such acting roles as Adam in *As You Like It* and the Ghost in *Hamlet*, a modest place on the stage that suggests that he may have had other duties in the management of the company. Such conclusions, however, are based on surmise.

What we do know is that his plays were popular and that he was highly successful in his vocation. His first play may have been *The Comedy of Errors*, acted perhaps in 1591. Certainly this was one of his earliest plays. The three parts of *Henry VI* were acted sometime between 1590 and 1592. Critics are not in agreement about precisely how much Shakespeare wrote of these three plays. *Richard III* probably dates from 1593. With this play Shakespeare captured the imagination of Elizabethan audiences, then enormously interested in historical plays. With *Richard III* Shakespeare also gave an interpretation pleasing to the Tudors of the rise to power of the grandfather of Queen Elizabeth. From this time onward, Shakespeare's plays followed on the stage in rapid succession: *Titus Andronicus, The Taming of the Shrew, The Two Gentlemen of Verona, Love's Labor's Lost, Romeo and Juliet, Richard II, A Midsummer Night's Dream, King John, The Merchant of Venice, Henry IV (Parts 1 and 2), Much Ado about Nothing, Henry V, Julius Cæsar, As You Like It, Twelfth Night, Hamlet, The Merry Wives of Windsor, All's Well That Ends Well, Measure for Measure, Othello, King Lear,* and nine others that followed before Shakespeare retired completely, about 1613.

In the course of his career in London, he made enough money to enable him to retire to Stratford with a competence. His purchase on May 4, 1597, of New Place, then the second-largest dwelling in Stratford, a "pretty house of brick and timber," with a handsome garden, indicates his increasing prosperity. There his wife and children lived while he busied himself in the London theatres. The summer before he acquired New Place, his life was darkened by the death of his only son, Hamnet, a child of eleven. In May, 1602, Shakespeare purchased one hundred and seven acres of fertile farmland near Stratford and a few months later bought a cottage and garden across the alley from New Place. About 1611, he seems to have returned permanently to Stratford, for the next year a legal document refers to him as "William Shakespeare of Stratford-upon-Avon . . . gentleman." To achieve the desired appellation of gentleman, William Shakespeare had seen to it that the College of Heralds in 1596 granted his father a coat of arms. In one step he thus became a second-generation gentleman.

Shakespeare's daughter Susanna made a good match in 1607 with Dr. John Hall, a prominent and prosperous Stratford physician. His second daughter, Judith, did not marry until she was thirty-two years old, and then, under somewhat scandalous circumstances, she married Thomas Quiney, a Stratford vintner. On March 25, 1616, Shakespeare made his will, bequeathing his landed property to Susanna, £300 to Judith, certain sums to other relatives, and his second-best bed to his wife, Anne. Much has been made of the second-best bed, but the legacy probably indicates only that Anne liked that particular bed. Shakespeare, following the practice of the time, may have already arranged with Susanna for his wife's care. Finally, on April 23, 1616, the anniversary of his birth, William Shakespeare died, and he was buried on April 25 within the chancel of Trinity Church, as befitted an honored citizen. On August 6, 1623, a few months before the publication of the collected edition of Shakespeare's plays, Anne Shakespeare joined her husband in death.

During his lifetime Shakespeare made no effort to publish any of his plays, though eighteen appeared in print in single-play editions known as quartos. Some of these are corrupt versions known as "bad quartos." No quarto, so far as is known, had the author's approval. Plays were not considered "literature" any more than most radio and television scripts today are considered literature. Dramatists sold their plays outright to the theatrical companies and it was usually considered in the company's interest to keep plays from getting into print. To achieve a reputation as a man of letters, Shakespeare wrote his *Sonnets* and his narrative poems, *Venus and Adonis* and *The Rape of Lucrece*, but he probably never dreamed that his plays would establish his reputation as a literary genius. Only Ben Jonson, a man known for his colossal conceit, had the crust to call his plays *Works*, as he did when he published an edition in 1616. But men laughed at Ben Jonson.

After Shakespeare's death, two of his old colleagues in the King's Men, John Heminges and Henry Condell, decided that it would be a good thing to print, in more accurate versions than were then available, the plays already published and eighteen additional plays not previously published in quarto. In 1623 appeared *Mr. William Shakespeares Comedies, Histories, & Tragedies. Published according to the True Originall Copies. Lon-*

don. Printed by Isaac Iaggard and Ed. Blount. This was the famous First Folio, a work that had the authority of Shakespeare's associates. The only play commonly attributed to Shakespeare that was omitted in the First Folio was *Pericles*. In their preface, "To the great Variety of Readers," Heminges and Condell state that whereas "you were abused with diverse stolen and surreptitious copies, maimed and deformed by the frauds and stealths of injurious impostors that exposed them, even those are now offered to your view cured and perfect of their limbs; and all the rest, absolute in their numbers, as he conceived them." What they used for printer's copy is one of the vexed problems of scholarship, and skilled bibliographers have devoted years of study to the question of the relation of the "copy" for the First Folio to Shakespeare's manuscripts. In some cases it is clear that the editors corrected printed quarto versions of the plays, probably by comparison with playhouse scripts. Whether these scripts were in Shakespeare's autograph is anybody's guess. No manuscript of any play in Shakespeare's handwriting has survived. Indeed, very few play manuscripts from this period by any author are extant. The Tudor and Stuart periods had not yet learned to prize autographs and authors' original manuscripts.

Since the First Folio contains eighteen plays not previously printed, it is the only source for these. For the other eighteen, which had appeared in quarto versions, the First Folio also has the authority of an edition prepared and overseen by Shakespeare's colleagues and professional associates. But since editorial standards in 1623 were far from strict, and Heminges and Condell were actors rather than editors by profession, the texts are sometimes careless. The printing and proofreading of the First Folio also left much to be desired, and some garbled passages have had to be corrected and emended. The "good quarto" texts have to be taken into account in preparing a modern edition.

Because of the great popularity of Shakespeare through the centuries, the First Folio has become a prized book, but it is not a very rare one, for it is estimated that 238 copies are extant. The Folger Shakespeare Library in Washington, D.C., has seventy-nine copies of the First Folio, collected by the founder, Henry Clay Folger, who believed that a collation of as many texts as possible would reveal significant facts about the text of Shakespeare's plays. Dr. Charlton Hinman, using an ingenious machine of his own invention for mechanical collating, has made many discoveries that throw light on Shakespeare's text and on printing practices of the day.

The probability is that the First Folio of 1623 had an edition of between 1,000 and 1,250 copies. It is believed that it sold for £1, which made it an expensive book, for £1 in 1623 was equivalent to something between $40 and $50 in modern purchasing power.

During the seventeenth century, Shakespeare was

sufficiently popular to warrant three later editions in folio size, the Second Folio of 1632, the Third Folio of 1663–1664, and the Fourth Folio of 1685. The Third Folio added six other plays ascribed to Shakespeare, but these are apocryphal.

THE SHAKESPEAREAN THEATRE

The theatres in which Shakespeare's plays were performed were vastly different from those we know today. The stage was a platform that jutted out into the area now occupied by the first rows of seats on the main floor, what is called the "orchestra" in America and the "pit" in England. This platform had no curtain to come down at the ends of acts and scenes. And although simple stage properties were available, the Elizabethan theatre lacked both the machinery and the elaborate movable scenery of the modern theatre. In the rear of the platform stage was a curtained area that could be used as an inner room, a tomb, or any such scene that might be required. A balcony above this inner room, and perhaps balconies on the sides of the stage, could represent the upper deck of a ship, the entry to Juliet's room, or a prison window. A trap door in the stage provided an entrance for ghosts and devils from the nether regions, and a similar trap in the canopied structure over the stage, known as the "heavens," made it possible to let down angels on a rope. These primitive stage arrangements help to account for many elements in Elizabethan plays. For example, since there was no curtain, the dramatist frequently felt the necessity of writing into his play action to clear the stage at the ends of acts and scenes. The funeral march at the end of *Hamlet* is not there merely for atmosphere; Shakespeare had to get the corpses off the stage. The lack of scenery also freed the dramatist from undue concern about the exact location of his sets, and the physical relation of his various settings to each other did not have to be worked out with the same precision as in the modern theatre.

Before London had buildings designed exclusively for theatrical entertainment, plays were given in inns and taverns. The characteristic inn of the period had an inner courtyard with rooms opening onto balconies overlooking the yard. Players could set up their temporary stages at one end of the yard and audiences could find seats on the balconies out of the weather. The poorer sort could stand or sit on the cobblestones in the yard, which was open to the sky. The first theatres followed this construction, and throughout the Elizabethan period the large public theatres had a yard in front of the stage open to the weather, with two or three tiers of covered balconies extending around the theatre. This physical structure again influenced the writing of plays. Because a dramatist wanted the actors to be heard, he frequently wrote into his play orations that could be delivered with declamatory effect. He also provided spectacle, buffoonery, and broad jests to keep the riotous groundlings in the yard entertained and quiet.

In another respect the Elizabethan theatre differed greatly from ours. It had no actresses. All women's roles were taken by boys, sometimes recruited from the boys' choirs of the London churches. Some of these youths acted their roles with great skill and the Elizabethans did not seem to be aware of any incongruity. The first actresses on the professional English stage appeared after the Restoration of Charles II, in 1660, when exiled Englishmen brought back from France practices of the French stage.

London in the Elizabethan period, as now, was the center of theatrical interest, though wandering actors from time to time traveled through the country performing in inns, halls, and the houses of the nobility. The first professional playhouse, called simply The Theatre, was erected by James Burbage, father of Shakespeare's colleague Richard Burbage, in 1576 on lands of the old Holywell Priory adjacent to Finsbury Fields, a playground and park area just north of the city walls. It had the advantage of being outside the city's jurisdiction and yet was near enough to be easily accessible. Soon after The Theatre was opened, another playhouse called The Curtain was erected in the same neighborhood. Both of these playhouses had open courtyards and were probably polygonal in shape.

About the time The Curtain opened, Richard Farrant, Master of the Children of the Chapel

Royal at Windsor and of St. Paul's, conceived the idea of opening a "private" theatre in the old monastery buildings of the Blackfriars, not far from St. Paul's Cathedral in the heart of the city. This theatre was ostensibly to train the choirboys in plays for presentation at Court, but Farrant managed to present plays to paying audiences and achieved considerable success until aristocratic neighbors complained and had the theatre closed. This first Blackfriars Theatre was significant, however, because it popularized the boy actors in a professional way and it paved the way for a second theatre in the Blackfriars, which Shakespeare's company took over more than thirty years later. By the last years of the sixteenth century, London had at least six professional theatres and still others were erected during the reign of James I.

The Globe Theatre, the playhouse that most people connect with Shakespeare, was erected early in 1599 on the Bankside, the area across the Thames from the city. Its construction had a dramatic beginning, for on the night of December 28, 1598, James Burbage's sons, Cuthbert and Richard, gathered together a crew who tore down the old theatre in Holywell and carted the timbers across the river to a site that they had chosen for a new playhouse. The reason for this clandestine operation was a row with the landowner over the lease to the Holywell property. The site chosen for the Globe was another playground outside of the city's jurisdiction, a region of somewhat unsavory character.

The Globe Playhouse.
From Visscher's *View of London* (1616).

Not far away was the Bear Garden, an amphitheatre devoted to the baiting of bears and bulls. This was also the region occupied by many houses of ill fame licensed by the Bishop of Winchester and the source of substantial revenue to him. But it was easily accessible either from London Bridge or by means of the cheap boats operated by the London watermen, and it had the great advantage of being beyond the authority of the Puritanical aldermen of London, who frowned on plays because they lured apprentices from work, filled their heads with improper ideas, and generally exerted a bad influence. The aldermen also complained that the crowds drawn together in the theatre helped to spread the plague.

The Globe was the handsomest theatre up to its time. It was a large building, apparently octagonal in shape, and open like its predecessors to the sky in the center, but capable of seating a large audience in its covered balconies. To erect and operate the Globe, the Burbages organized a syndicate composed of the leading members of the dramatic company, of which Shakespeare was a member. Since it was open to the weather and depended on natural light, plays had to be given in the afternoon. This caused no hardship in the long afternoons of an English summer, but in the winter the weather was a great handicap and discouraged all except the hardiest. For that reason, in 1608 Shakespeare's company was glad to take over the lease of the second Blackfriars Theatre, a substantial, roomy hall reconstructed within the framework of the old monastery building. This theatre was protected from the weather and its stage was artificially lighted by chandeliers of candles. This became the winter playhouse for Shakespeare's company and at once proved so popular that the congestion of traffic created an embarrassing problem. Stringent regulations had to be made for the movement of coaches in the vicinity. Shakespeare's company continued to use the Globe during the summer months. In 1613 a squib fired from a cannon during a performance of *Henry VIII* fell on the thatched roof and the Globe burned to the ground. The next year it was rebuilt.

London had other famous theatres. The Rose, just west of the Globe, was built by Philip Henslowe, a semiliterate denizen of the Bankside, who became one of the most important theatrical owners and producers of the Tudor and Stuart periods. What is more important for historians, he kept a detailed account book, which provides much of our information about theatrical history in his time. Another famous theatre on the Bankside was the Swan, which a Dutch priest, Johannes de Witt, visited in 1596. The crude drawing of the stage which he made was copied by his friend Arend van Buchell; it is one of the important pieces of contemporary evidence for theatrical construction. Among the other theatres, the Fortune, north of the city, on Golding Lane, and the Red Bull, even farther away from the city, off St. John's Street, were the most popular. The Red Bull, much frequented by apprentices, favored sensational and sometimes rowdy plays.

The actors who kept all of these theatres going were organized into companies under the protection of some noble patron. Traditionally actors had enjoyed a low reputation. In some of the ordinances they were classed as vagrants; in the phraseology of the time, "rogues, vagabonds, sturdy beggars, and common players" were all listed together as undesirables. To escape penalties often meted out to these characters, organized groups of actors managed to gain the protection of various personages of high degree. In the later years of Elizabeth's reign, a group flourished under the name of the Queen's Men; another group had the protection of the Lord Admiral and were known as the Lord Admiral's Men. Edward Alleyn, son-in-law of Philip Henslowe, was the leading spirit in the Lord Admiral's Men. Besides the adult companies, troupes of boy actors from time to time also enjoyed considerable popularity. Among these were the Children of Paul's and the Children of the Chapel Royal.

The company with which Shakespeare had a long association had for its first patron Henry Carey, Lord Hunsdon, the Lord Chamberlain, and hence they were known as the Lord Chamberlain's Men. After the accession of James I, they became the King's Men. This company was the great rival of the Lord Admiral's Men, managed by Henslowe and Alleyn.

All was not easy for the players in Shakespeare's time, for the aldermen of London were always eager for an excuse to close up the Blackfriars and any other theatres in their jurisdiction. The theatres outside the jurisdiction of London were not immune from interference, for they might be shut up by order of the Privy Council for meddling in politics or for various other offenses, or they might be closed in time of plague lest they spread infection. During plague times, the actors usually went on tour and played the provinces wherever they could find an audience. Particularly frightening were the plagues of 1592–1594 and 1613 when the theatres closed and the players, like many other Londoners, had to take to the country.

Though players had a low social status, they enjoyed great popularity, and one of the favorite forms of entertainment at court was the performance of plays. To be commanded to perform at court conferred great prestige upon a company of players, and printers frequently noted that fact when they published plays. Several of Shakespeare's plays were performed before the sovereign, and Shakespeare himself undoubtedly acted in some of these plays.

REFERENCES FOR FURTHER READING

Many readers will want suggestions for further reading about Shakespeare and his times. The literature in this field is enormous but a few references will serve as guides to further study. A simple and useful little book is Gerald Sanders, *A Shakespeare Primer* (New York, 1950). *A Companion to Shakespeare Studies*, edited by Harley Granville-Barker and G. B. Harrison (Cambridge, Eng., 1934), is a valuable guide. More detailed but still not so voluminous as to be confusing is Hazelton Spencer, *The Art and Life of William Shakespeare* (New York, 1940), which, like Sanders' handbook, contains a brief annotated list of useful books on various aspects of the subject. The most recent concise handbook of facts about Shakespeare is Gerald E. Bentley, *Shakespeare: A Biographical Handbook* (New Haven, 1961). The most detailed and scholarly work providing complete factual information about Shakespeare is Sir Edmund Chambers, *William Shakespeare: A Study of Facts and Problems* (2 vols., Oxford, 1930). For detailed, factual information about the Elizabethan and seventeenth-century stages, the definitive reference works are Sir Edmund Chambers, *The Elizabethan Stage* (4 vols., Oxford, 1923) and Gerald E. Bentley, *The Jacobean and Caroline Stage* (5 vols., Oxford, 1941–1956). Alfred Harbage, *Shakespeare's Audience* (New York, 1941) throws light on the nature and tastes for the customers for whom Elizabethan dramatists wrote.

Although specialists disagree about the details of stage construction, the reader will find essential information in John C. Adams, *The Globe Playhouse: Its Design and Equipment* (Cambridge, Mass., 1942; 2nd ed., rev., New York, 1961). A model of the Globe playhouse by Dr. Adams is on permanent exhibition in the Folger Shakespeare Library in Washington, D.C. An excellent description of the architecture of the Globe is Irwin Smith, *Shakespeare's Globe Playhouse: A Modern Reconstruction in Text and Scale Drawings Based upon the Reconstruction of the Globe by John Cranford Adams* (New York, 1956). Another recent study of the physical characteristics of the Globe is C. Walter Hodges, *The Globe Restored* (London, 1953). An easily read history of the early theatres is J. Q. Adams, *Shakespearean Playhouses: A History of English Theatres from the Beginnings to the Restoration* (Boston, 1917). Bernard Beckerman, *Shakespeare at the Globe, 1599–1609* (New York, 1962), considers, in addition to the physical conditions of Shakespeare's theatre, theatrical conventions and acting styles of the period.

The following titles on theatrical history will provide information about Shakespeare's plays in later periods: Alfred Harbage, *Theatre for Shakespeare* (Toronto, 1955); Esther Cloudman Dunn, *Shakespeare in America* (New York, 1939); George C. D. Odell, *Shakespeare from Betterton to Irving* (2 vols.,

London, 1931); Arthur Colby Sprague, *Shakespeare and the Actors: The Stage Business in His Plays (1660–1905)* (Cambridge, Mass., 1944) and *Shakespearian Players and Performances* (Cambridge, Mass., 1953); Leslie Hotson, *The Commonwealth and Restoration Stage* (Cambridge, Mass., 1928); Alwin Thaler, *Shakspere to Sheridan: A Book About the Theatre of Yesterday and To-day* (Cambridge, Mass., 1922); and Ernest Bradlee Watson, *Sheridan to Robertson: A Study of the 19th-Century London Stage* (Cambridge, Mass., 1926). Enid Welsford, *The Court Masque* (Cambridge, Mass., 1927) is an excellent study of the characteristics of this form of entertainment.

Harley Granville-Barker, *Prefaces to Shakespeare* (5 vols., London, 1927–1948) provides stimulating critical discussion of the plays. An older classic of criticism is Andrew C. Bradley, *Shakespearean Tragedy: Lectures on Hamlet, Othello, King Lear, Macbeth* (London, 1904), which is now available in an inexpensive reprint (New York, 1955). Thomas M. Parrott, *Shakespearean Comedy* (New York, 1949) is scholarly and readable. Also useful are George S. Gordon, *Shakespearian Comedy and Other Studies* (London and New York, 1945) and John R. Brown, *Shakespeare and His Comedies* (London, 1957). Shakespeare's dramatizations of English history are examined in E. M. W. Tillyard, *Shakespeare's History Plays* (London, 1948), and Lily Bess Campbell, *Shakespeare's "Histories," Mirrors of Elizabethan Policy* (San Marino, Calif., 1947) contains a more technical discussion of the same subject. Although Edward Dowden's criticism is no longer fashionable, his *Shakspere: A Critical Study of His Mind and Art* (London, 1901; paperback reprint, 1962) is sensitive and often sensible. Sir Edmund Chambers, *Shakespeare: A Survey* (London, 1925; paperback reprint, 1958 [?]), contains brief but illuminating comment on each of the plays.

The most recent edition of *The Comedy of Errors* is that by R. A. Foakes in the new "Arden" series (London, 1962), which contains detailed critical comment. Further discussion will be found in the general works on Shakespeare's comedies listed above. Harold Brooks, "Themes and Structure in 'The Comedy of Errors,'" in *Early Shakespeare*, ed. John R. Brown and Bernard Harris (London, 1961), pp. 55-71, contains a valuable analysis of the action of the play and the manner in which Shakespeare used his sources to emphasize certain themes.

The question of the authenticity of Shakespeare's plays arouses perennial attention. A book that demolishes the notion of hidden cryptograms in the plays is William F. Friedman and Elizebeth S. Friedman, *The Shakespearean Ciphers Examined* (New York, 1957). A succinct account of the various absurdities advanced to suggest the authorship of a multitude of candidates other than Shakespeare will be found in R. C. Churchill's *Shakespeare and His Betters* (Bloomington, Ind., 1959) and Frank W. Wadsworth, *The Poacher from Stratford: A Partial Account of the Controversy over the Authorship of Shakespeare's Plays* (Berkeley, Calif., 1958). An essay on the curious notions in the writings of the anti-Shakespeareans is that by Louis B. Wright, "The Anti-Shakespeare Industry and the Growth of Cults," *The Virginia Quarterly Review*, XXXV (1959), pp. 289-303. Another recent discussion of the subject, *The Authorship of Shakespeare*, by James G. McManaway (Washington, 1962), presents all the evidence from contemporary records to prove the identity of Shakespeare the actor-playwright with Shakespeare of Stratford.

Reprints of some of the sources of Shakespeare's plays can be found in *Shakespeare's Library* (2 vols., 1850), edited by John Payne Collier, and *The Shakespeare Classics* (12 vols., 1907–1926), edited by Israel Gollancz. Geoffrey Bullough, *Narrative and Dramatic Sources of Shakespeare* contains the most recent reprinting of the source narratives (4 volumes published to date, covering the comedies written before 1603 and the history plays). For discussion of Shakespeare's use of his sources see Kenneth Muir, *Shakespeare's Sources: Comedies and Tragedies* (London, 1957). Thomas M. Cranfill has edited a facsimile reprint of Barnabe Rich's *Farewell to Military Profession (1581)* (Austin, Tex., 1959), which contains stories that Shakespeare probably used for several of his plays.

Interesting pictures as well as new information about Shakespeare will be found in F. E. Halliday, *Shakespeare, a Pictorial Biography* (London, 1956).

Allardyce Nicoll, *The Elizabethans* (Cambridge, Eng., 1957) contains a variety of illustrations.

A brief, clear, and accurate account of Tudor history is S. T. Bindoff, *The Tudors,* in the Penguin series. A readable general history is G. M. Trevelyan, *The History of England,* first published in 1926 and available in many editions. G. M. Trevelyan, *English Social History,* first published in 1942 and also available in many editions, provides fascinating information about England in all periods. Sir John Neale, *Queen Elizabeth* (London, 1934) is the best study of the great Queen. Various aspects of life in the Elizabethan period are treated in Louis B. Wright, *Middle-Class Culture in Elizabethan England* (Chapel Hill, N.C.; reprinted Ithaca, N.Y., 1958). *Shakespeare's England: An Account of the Life and Manners of His Age,* edited by Sidney Lee and C. T. Onions (2 vols., Oxford, 1916), provides a large amount of information on many aspects of life in the Elizabethan period. Additional information will be found in Muriel St. C. Byrne, *Elizabethan Life in Town and Country* (London, 1925; rev. ed., 1954; paperback, N.Y., 1961).

The Folger Shakespeare Library is currently publishing a series of illustrated pamphlets on various aspects of English life in the sixteenth and seventeenth centuries. The following titles have been published: Dorothy E. Mason, *Music in Elizabethan England;* Craig R. Thompson, *The English Church in the Sixteenth Century;* Louis B. Wright, *Shakespeare's Theatre and the Dramatic Tradition;* Giles

E. Dawson, *The Life of William Shakespeare;* Virginia A. LaMar, *English Dress in the Age of Shakespeare;* Craig R. Thompson, *The Bible in English, 1525–1611, The English Church in the Sixteenth Century, Schools in Tudor England,* and *Universities in Tudor England;* Lilly C. Stone, *English Sports and Recreations;* Conyers Read, *The Government of England under Elizabeth;* Virginia A. LaMar, *Travel and Roads in England;* John R. Hale, *The Art of War and Renaissance England;* Albert J. Schmidt, *The Yeoman in Tudor and Stuart England;* James G. McManaway, *The Authorship of Shakespeare;* Boies Penrose, *Tudor and Early Stuart Voyaging;* and Garrett Mattingly, *The "Invincible" Armada and Elizabethan England.*

[*Dramatis Personae*

Solinus, Duke of Ephesus.

Egeon, a merchant of Syracuse.

Antipholus of Ephesus, } twin brothers and sons to
Antipholus of Syracuse, }   *Egeon* and *Emilia*.

Dromio of Ephesus, } twin brothers and attendants on the
Dromio of Syracuse, }   two *Antipholuses*.

Balthazar, a merchant.

Angelo, a goldsmith.

First Merchant, friend to *Antipholus of Syracuse*.

Second Merchant, to whom *Angelo* is debtor.

Pinch, a schoolmaster.

Emilia, an abbess of Ephesus, wife to *Egeon*.

Adriana, wife to *Antipholus of Ephesus*.

Luciana, her sister.

Luce, servant to *Adriana*.

A Courtesan.

       Jailer, Officers, and other Attendants.

         SCENE: *Ephesus*.]

THE COMEDY
OF ERRORS

ACT I

I. i. The scene opens in Ephesus, as Egeon, a merchant of Syracuse, has just received a death sentence unless he can pay a fine of 1,000 marks. Enmity between Ephesus and Syracuse has resulted in the imposition of such penalties upon merchants of one city who visit the other. In answer to the Duke's question as to his business in Ephesus, Egeon relates this story: The ship that was taking him, his wife and twin sons, and the twin sons of a servant woman from Epidamnum to Syracuse foundered in a storm. He and one of each pair of twins were rescued separately from his wife and the other two boys, who were carried to another port. After eighteen years his son begged to be allowed to seek his brother and set out accompanied by his servant, the other twin. For the past five years he (Egeon) has traveled all over Greece seeking his lost family. Egeon's story moves the compassionate Duke of Ephesus. Although he cannot revoke the penalty, he grants Egeon a day to seek the necessary sum to save his life.

⎯⎯⎯⎯⎯⎯⎯⎯⎯⎯⎯⎯⎯

2. **doom:** sentence.
8. **wanting:** lacking.
9. **sealed:** confirmed.
11. **mortal and intestine: mortal** in the sense "fatal," which **intestine** reinforces, though it means at the same time "internal, domestic"; **jars:** broils; dissensions.
12. **seditious:** turbulent; quarrelsome.

Scene I. [A hall in the Duke's palace.]

*Enter [Solinus], the Duke of Ephesus, with [Egeon],
the merchant of Syracuse, Jailer, and other
Attendants.*

  Ege. Proceed, Solinus, to procure my fall,
And by the doom of death end woes and all.
  Duke. Merchant of Syracusa, plead no more:
I am not partial to infringe our laws.
The enmity and discord which of late   5
Sprung from the rancorous outrage of your duke
To merchants, our well-dealing countrymen,
Who, wanting guilders to redeem their lives,
Have sealed his rigorous statutes with their bloods,
Excludes all pity from our threat'ning looks.   10
For, since the mortal and intestine jars
'Twixt thy seditious countrymen and us,
It hath in solemn synods been decreed,
Both by the Syracusians and ourselves,
To admit no traffic to our adverse towns.   15
Nay, more, if any born at Ephesus be seen
At any Syracusian marts and fairs—
Again, if any Syracusian born

22. **quit:** satisfy; meet by payment.

35. **nature:** i.e., natural behavior (in seeking his family).

36. **what my sorrow gives me leave:** as much as grief will let me utter.

39. **hap:** fortune.

42. **factor:** agent.

43. **at random:** unheeded.

Come to the Bay of Ephesus—he dies,
His goods confiscate to the Duke's dispose,   20
Unless a thousand marks be levied,
To quit the penalty and to ransom him.
Thy substance, valued at the highest rate,
Cannot amount unto a hundred marks;
Therefore by law thou art condemned to die.   25
 Ege. Yet this my comfort: when your words are
  done,
My woes end likewise with the evening sun.
 Duke. Well, Syracusian, say in brief the cause
Why thou departedst from thy native home   30
And for what cause thou camest to Ephesus.
 Ege. A heavier task could not have been imposed
Than I to speak my griefs unspeakable:
Yet, that the world may witness that my end
Was wrought by nature, not by vile offense,   35
I'll utter what my sorrow gives me leave.
In Syracusa was I born and wed
Unto a woman, happy but for me,
And by me too, had not our hap been bad.
With her I lived in joy; our wealth increased   40
By prosperous voyages I often made
To Epidamnum, till my factor's death
And the great care of goods at random left
Drew me from kind embracements of my spouse:
From whom my absence was not six months old   45
Before herself, almost at fainting under
The pleasing punishment that women bear,
Had made provision for her following me

55. **meaner:** of poorer birth.

59. **not meanly proud:** not moderately proud; i.e., exceedingly proud.

60. **motions:** proposals.

65. **tragic instance of our harm:** i.e., sign of causing us tragic harm.

69. **doubtful:** dreadful.

74. **for fashion:** in the manner of infants.

And soon and safe arrived where I was.
There had she not been long but she became   50
A joyful mother of two goodly sons;
And, which was strange, the one so like the other
As could not be distinguished but by names.
That very hour, and in the selfsame inn,
A meaner woman was delivered   55
Of such a burden, male twins, both alike:
Those, for their parents were exceeding poor,
I bought and brought up to attend my sons.
My wife, not meanly proud of two such boys,
Made daily motions for our home return.   60
Unwilling, I agreed; alas! too soon
We came aboard.
A league from Epidamnum had we sailed
Before the always-wind-obeying deep
Gave any tragic instance of our harm: 65
But longer did we not retain much hope;
For what obscured light the heavens did grant
Did but convey unto our fearful minds
A doubtful warrant of immediate death,
Which though myself would gladly have embraced,   70
Yet the incessant weepings of my wife,
Weeping before for what she saw must come,
And piteous plainings of the pretty babes,
That mourned for fashion, ignorant what to fear,
Forced me to seek delays for them and me.   75
And this it was, for other means was none:
The sailors sought for safety by our boat,
And left the ship, then sinking-ripe, to us.

85. **on whom:** on the child on whom.
87. **straight:** at once.
93. **amain:** at full speed.
96. **that:** what (that which).

My wife, more careful for the latter-born,
Had fastened him unto a small spare mast,   80
Such as seafaring men provide for storms;
To him one of the other twins was bound,
Whilst I had been like heedful of the other.
The children thus disposed, my wife and I,
Fixing our eyes on whom our care was fixed,   85
Fastened ourselves at either end the mast,
And, floating straight, obedient to the stream,
Was carried towards Corinth, as we thought.
At length the sun, gazing upon the earth,
Dispersed those vapors that offended us;   90
And, by the benefit of his wished light,
The seas waxed calm and we discovered
Two ships from far, making amain to us,
Of Corinth that, of Epidaurus this.
But ere they came—O, let me say no more!   95
Gather the sequel by that went before.
    Duke. Nay, forward, old man, do not break off so;
For we may pity though not pardon thee.
    Ege. O, had the gods done so, I had not now
Worthily termed them merciless to us!   100
For, ere the ships could meet by twice five leagues
We were encountered by a mighty rock,
Which being violently borne upon,
Our helpful ship was splitted in the midst;
So that, in this unjust divorce of us   105
Fortune had left to both of us alike
What to delight in, what to sorrow for.
Her part, poor soul, seeming as burdened

115. **healthful welcome:** rescue.

116. **would have reft the fishers of their prey:** i.e., would have intercepted his wife and the other two children in the Corinth fishermen's vessel.

120. **That:** so that.

123. **dilate at full:** describe fully.

131–32. **Whom whilst I labored of a love to see,/I hazarded the loss of whom I loved:** that is, for whom my love made me grieve and for whose sake I hazarded the loss of my other loved son.

With lesser weight, but not with lesser woe,
Was carried with more speed before the wind;   110
And in our sight they three were taken up
By fishermen of Corinth, as we thought.
At length another ship had seized on us,
And, knowing whom it was their hap to save,
Gave healthful welcome to their shipwracked guests 115
And would have reft the fishers of their prey,
Had not their bark been very slow of sail;
And therefore homeward did they bend their course.
Thus have you heard me severed from my bliss,
That by misfortunes was my life prolonged,   120
To tell sad stories of my own mishaps.
    Duke. And, for the sake of them thou sorrowest for,
Do me the favor to dilate at full
What hath befall'n of them and thee till now.
    Ege. My youngest boy, and yet my eldest care,   125
At eighteen years became inquisitive
After his brother and importuned me
That his attendant—so his case was like,
Reft of his brother, but retained his name—
Might bear him company in the quest of him: 130
Whom whilst I labored of a love to see,
I hazarded the loss of whom I loved.
Five summers have I spent in farthest Greece,
Roaming clean through the bounds of Asia,
And, coasting homeward, came to Ephesus;   135
Hopeless to find, yet loath to leave unsought
Or that or any place that harbors men.
But here must end the story of my life;

139. **timely:** early.

140. **travels:** painful travels. **Travels** and "travails" were not two distinct words.

The three Fates. From Vincenzo Cartari, *Imagini delli dei degl' antichi* (1674).

6

And happy were I in my timely death,
Could all my travels warrant me they live.   140
　　Duke. Hapless Egeon, whom the Fates have
　　marked
To bear the extremity of dire mishap!
Now, trust me, were it not against our laws,
Against my crown, my oath, my dignity,   145
Which princes, would they, may not disannul,
My soul should sue as advocate for thee.
But, though thou art adjudged to the death,
And passed sentence may not be recalled
But to our honor's great disparagement,   150
Yet will I favor thee in what I can.
Therefore, merchant, I'll limit thee this day
To seek thy health by beneficial help.
Try all the friends thou hast in Ephesus;
Beg thou, or borrow, to make up the sum   155
And live; if no, then thou art doomed to die.
Jailer, take him to thy custody.
　　Jail. I will, my lord.
　　Ege. Hopeless and helpless doth Egeon wend,
But to procrastinate his lifeless end.   160
　　　　　　　　　　　　　　Exeunt.

I. [ii.] Antipholus of Syracuse is warned by another merchant to conceal his place of origin for fear of the penalty that has been invoked on another Syracusan merchant that very day. Sending his servant, Dromio, to their inn to leave his money in safekeeping, Antipholus decides to view the city of Ephesus. He expects no pleasure from the visit, because his spirits are wholly dedicated to the search for his mother and missing brother. Meeting Dromio of Ephesus, he is surprised at what appears to be the quick return of his servant, not knowing that this is the twin brother of his servant, one who attends his lost brother, Antipholus of Ephesus. The Ephesian Antipholus is married and his wife has sent Dromio to bid her husband home to supper. Antipholus of Syracuse, on the other hand, knows nothing of any wife and questions Dromio fruitlessly about the safety of the money which he thinks he has entrusted to him. When in exasperation he begins to strike Dromio, the servant takes to his heels and Antipholus sets out for the inn to satisfy himself that his money is safe.

ıııııııııııııııııııııııııııııııııııı

9. **host:** lodge.
18. **so good a mean:** such a sum of money.

[Scene II. The mart.]

*Enter Antipholus [of Syracuse], a Merchant [of
    Ephesus], and Dromio [of Syracuse].*

Mer. Therefore give out you are of Epidamnum,
Lest that your goods too soon be confiscate.
This very day a Syracusian merchant
Is apprehended for arrival here;
And, not being able to buy out his life,   5
According to the statute of the town,
Dies ere the weary sun set in the West.
There is your money that I had to keep.
S. Ant. Go bear it to the Centaur, where we host,
And stay there, Dromio, till I come to thee.   10
Within this hour it will be dinnertime:
Till that, I'll view the manners of the town,
Peruse the traders, gaze upon the buildings,
And then return and sleep within mine inn;
For with long travel I am stiff and weary.   15
Get thee away.
S. Dro. Many a man would take you at your word
And go indeed, having so good a mean.   *Exit.*
S. Ant. A trusty villain, sir, that very oft,
When I am dull with care and melancholy,   20
Lightens my humor with his merry jests.
What, will you walk with me about the town,
And then go to my inn and dine with me?
Mer. I am invited, sir, to certain merchants,

27. **Please you:** if it please you.

29. **present:** immediate.

32. **commend you to your own content:** leave you to your pleasure.

38. **confounds:** loses.

41. **almanac:** i.e., reminder (since Dromio was born at the same hour as his master); **date:** date of birth.

50. **stomach:** appetite.

An Elizabethan merchant. From Theodor de Bry, *Emblemata nobilitati et vulgo* (1593).

Of whom I hope to make much benefit: 25
I crave your pardon. Soon at five o'clock,
Please you, I'll meet with you upon the mart
And afterward consort you till bedtime.
My present business calls me from you now.

   S. Ant. Farewell till then: I will go lose myself   30
And wander up and down to view the city.

   Mer. Sir, I commend you to your own content.

                                    Exit.

   S. Ant. He that commends me to mine own content
Commends me to the thing I cannot get.
I to the world am like a drop of water   35
That in the ocean seeks another drop;
Who, falling there to find his fellow forth,
Unseen, inquisitive, confounds himself:
So I, to find a mother and a brother,
In quest of them, unhappy, lose myself.   40

       Enter Dromio of Ephesus.

Here comes the almanac of my true date.
What now? How chance thou art returned so soon?

   E. Dro. Returned so soon! Rather approached too
     late!
The capon burns, the pig falls from the spit;   45
The clock hath strucken twelve upon the bell;
My mistress made it one upon my cheek.
She is so hot because the meat is cold;
The meat is cold because you come not home;
You come not home because you have no stomach;   50

54. **Stop in your wind:** stop before you are winded.

64. **in post:** with posthaste speed.

65. **post:** the reference is to the keeping of tavern bills by scoring a post for food and drink dispensed to a customer.

66. **pate:** head.

67. **maw:** stomach.

69–70. **out of season:** inappropriate.

You have no stomach, having broke your fast;
But we, that know what 'tis to fast and pray,
Are penitent for your default today.

    S. Ant. Stop in your wind, sir: tell me this, I pray,
Where have you left the money that I gave you?   55

    E. Dro. O—sixpence, that I had o' Wednesday last
To pay the saddler for my mistress' crupper.
The saddler had it, sir; I kept it not.

    S. Ant. I am not in a sportive humor now.
Tell me, and dally not, where is the money?   60
We being strangers here, how darest thou trust
So great a charge from thine own custody?

    E. Dro. I pray you, jest, sir, as you sit at dinner:
I from my mistress come to you in post;
If I return, I shall be post indeed,   65
For she will score your fault upon my pate.
Methinks your maw, like mine, should be your clock
And strike you home without a messenger.

    S. Ant. Come, Dromio, come, these jests are out of
      season;   70
Reserve them till a merrier hour than this.
Where is the gold I gave in charge to thee?

    E. Dro. To me, sir? Why, you gave no gold to me.

    S. Ant. Come on, sir knave, have done your foolish-
      ness,   75
And tell me how thou hast disposed thy charge.

    E. Dro. My charge was but to fetch you from the
      mart
Home to your house, the Phoenix, sir, to dinner:
My mistress and her sister stays for you.   80

83. **sconce:** another jocular word for "head."

84. **stands:** insists; **undisposed:** not disposed to mirth.

103. **o'erraught:** overreached; cheated.

104. **cozenage:** trickery.

109. **liberties of sin:** tolerated sinners.

S. Ant. Now, as I am a Christian, answer me
In what safe place you have bestowed my money,
Or I shall break that merry sconce of yours,
That stands on tricks when I am undisposed.
Where is the thousand marks thou hadst of me?   85

 E. Dro. I have some marks of yours upon my pate,
Some of my mistress' marks upon my shoulders,
But not a thousand marks between you both.
If I should pay your Worship those again,
Perchance you will not bear them patiently.   90

 S. Ant. Thy mistress' marks? What mistress, slave,
  hast thou?

 E. Dro. Your Worship's wife, my mistress at the
  Phoenix;
She that doth fast till you come home to dinner,   95
And prays that you will hie you home to dinner.

 S. Ant. What, wilt thou flout me thus unto my face,
Being forbid? There, take you that, sir knave.

 E. Dro. What mean you, sir? For God's sake, hold
 your hands!   100
Nay, and you will not, sir, I'll take my heels.   *Exit.*

 S. Ant. Upon my life, by some device or other
The villain is o'erraught of all my money.
They say this town is full of cozenage,
As, nimble jugglers that deceive the eye,   105
Dark-working sorcerers that change the mind,
Soul-killing witches that deform the body,
Disguised cheaters, prating mountebanks,
And many suchlike liberties of sin:

A view of Ephesus in the seventeenth century. From George Wheler, *Voyage de Dalmatie, de Grèce, et du Levant* (1689).

If it prove so, I will be gone the sooner.   110
I'll to the Centaur to go seek this slave;
I greatly fear my money is not safe.

                                        Exit.

THE COMEDY
OF ERRORS

ACT II

II. [i.] Adriana, wife of Antipholus of Ephesus, impatiently awaits her husband's homecoming. When Dromio returns and reports Antipholus' reaction to his message, his refusal to come home and denial of even having a wife, Adriana bitterly comments on his neglect, which she fears may end in actual infidelity.

<hr/>

12. **Look when:** whenever.
17. **his bound:** its territory.

ACT II

*Enter Adriana, wife to Antipholus, with Luciana,
her sister.*

Adr. Neither my husband nor the slave returned
That in such haste I sent to seek his master!
Sure, Luciana, it is two o'clock.
　Luc. Perhaps some merchant hath invited him,
And from the mart he's somewhere gone to dinner.　5
Good sister, let us dine, and never fret;
A man is master of his liberty;
Time is their master and, when they see time,
They'll go or come; if so, be patient, sister.
　Adr. Why should their liberty than ours be more?　10
　Luc. Because their business still lies out o' door.
　Adr. Look when I serve him so, he takes it ill.
　Luc. O, know he is the bridle of your will.
　Adr. There's none but asses will be bridled so.
　Luc. Why, headstrong liberty is lashed with woe.　15
There's nothing situate under Heaven's eye
But hath his bound, in earth, in sea, in sky:

22. **Indued:** endowed.

25. **attend on their accords:** follow the example they set.

28–9. **bear some sway:** retain some authority.

31. **start:** stray.

32. **forbear:** be patient.

41. **helpless:** unhelpful.

43. **fool-begged patience:** patience carried to the point of idiocy. The reference is to applying to the Court of Wards for the guardianship of a minor on the grounds of mental incompetence. A minor so sued for was said to be "begged for a fool"; **left:** i.e., your only consolation, with a pun on **left** and **right.**

The beasts, the fishes, and the winged fowls
Are their males' subjects and at their controls.
Men, more divine, the masters of all these,   20
Lords of the wide world and wild watery seas,
Indued with intellectual sense and souls,
Of more preeminence than fish and fowls,
Are masters to their females and their lords:
Then let your will attend on their accords.   25

  Adr. This servitude makes you to keep unwed.
  Luc. Not this, but troubles of the marriage bed.
  Adr. But, were you wedded, you would bear some
    sway.
  Luc. Ere I learn love, I'll practice to obey.   30
  Adr. How if your husband start some other where?
  Luc. Till he come home again I would forbear.
  Adr. Patience unmoved! no marvel though she
    pause;
They can be meek that have no other cause.   35
A wretched soul, bruised with adversity,
We bid be quiet when we hear it cry;
But were we burdened with like weight of pain,
As much, or more, we should ourselves complain.
So thou, that hast no unkind mate to grieve thee,   40
With urging helpless patience would relieve me;
But if thou live to see like right bereft,
This fool-begged patience in thee will be left.
  Luc. Well, I will marry one day, but to try.
Here comes your man; now is your husband nigh.   45

52. **Beshrew:** plague take; **understand it:** a pun on "stand under it."

56. **doubtfully:** (1) unclearly; (2) dreadfully.

60–1. **horn-mad:** as mad as an enraged beast, with a quibble on the behavior of an animal in the rutting season.

62–3. **Horn-mad . . . cuckold-mad:** Adriana assumes that he means the word **horn-mad** in the sense "enraged at being made a cuckold." The reference would then be to the horns that were proverbially supposed to adorn the head of a man whose wife had been unfaithful.

Enter Dromio [of] Ephesus.

Adr. Say, is your tardy master now at hand?

E. Dro. Nay, he's at two hands with me, and that
my two ears can witness.

Adr. Say, didst thou speak with him? Knowst thou
    his mind?   50

E. Dro. Ay, ay, he told his mind upon mine ear:
Beshrew his hand, I scarce could understand it.

Luc. Spake he so doubtfully thou couldst not feel
his meaning?

E. Dro. Nay, he struck so plainly I could too well   55
feel his blows; and withal so doubtfully that I could
scarce understand them.

Adr. But say, I prithee, is he coming home?
It seems he hath great care to please his wife.

E. Dro. Why, mistress, sure my master is horn-   60
    mad.

Adr. Horn-mad, thou villain!

E. Dro.   I mean not cuckold-mad;
But, sure, he is stark mad.
When I desired him to come home to dinner,   65
He asked me for a thousand marks in gold.
"'Tis dinnertime," quoth I. "My gold!" quoth he.
"Your meat doth burn," quoth I. "My gold!" quoth he.
"Will you come home?" quoth I. "My gold!" quoth he;
"Where is the thousand marks I gave thee, villain?"   70
"The pig," quoth I, "is burned." "My gold!" quoth he.
"My mistress, sir," quoth I. "Hang up thy mistress!
I know not thy mistress; out on thy mistress!"

77–8. **my errand, due unto my tongue . . . I bare home upon my shoulders:** i.e., the reply consisted of a beating instead of a verbal message.

87. **holy:** a pun on "hole-y"; i.e., broken.

90. **Am I so round with you as you with me:** do I appear as **round** in shape as you are **round** (blunt) in speaking to me.

91. **spurn:** kick.

95. **minions:** paramours; **grace:** honor.

102. **bait:** lure.

A game of football. Note the round ball. From Henry Peacham, *Minerva Britanna* (1612).

Luc. Quoth who?

E. Dro.　　　　　Quoth my master: 75
"I know," quoth he, "no house, no wife, no mistress."
So that my errand, due unto my tongue,
I thank him, I bare home upon my shoulders;
For, in conclusion, he did beat me there.

Adr. Go back again, thou slave, and fetch him 80
　　home.

E. Dro. Go back again, and be new beaten home?
For God's sake, send some other messenger.

Adr. Back, slave, or I will break thy pate across.

E. Dro. And he will bless that cross with other 85
　　beating:
Between you I shall have a holy head.

Adr. Hence, prating peasant! Fetch thy master
　　home.

E. Dro. Am I so round with you as you with me, 90
That like a football you do spurn me thus?
You spurn me hence, and he will spurn me hither:
If I last in this service, you must case me in leather.
　　　　　　　　　　　　　　　　Exit.

Luc. Fie, how impatience lowereth in your face!

Adr. His company must do his minions grace, 95
Whilst I at home starve for a merry look.
Hath homely age the alluring beauty took
From my poor cheek? Then he hath wasted it.
Are my discourses dull? barren my wit?
If voluble and sharp discourse be marred, 100
Unkindness blunts it more than marble hard.
Do their gay vestments his affections bait?

105. **ground:** cause.

106. **defeatures:** disfigurements; **fair:** beauty.

108. **pale:** paling fence, such as enclosed a deer park.

109. **stale:** "A lover or mistress whose devotion is turned into ridicule for the amusement of a rival or rivals" (*Oxford Eng. Dict.*).

114. **what lets it but he would be here:** i.e., what hinders his coming.

118–22. **I . . . shame:** these lines have puzzled all editors and may contain some corruption, although it is possible that the confusion is a deliberate reflection of Adriana's jealous state of mind. She seems obsessed with the idea that she has lost her beauty and her husband's regard; at the same time she is bitter at what she considers his misconduct. She equates herself with a mere beautiful ornament, whose value depends on its fresh appearance, while her husband is like a gold coin, which does not depreciate in value despite much handling by many hands.

125. **fond:** foolish.

That's not my fault; he's master of my state.
What ruins are in me that can be found,
By him not ruined? Then is he the ground   105
Of my defeatures. My decayed fair
A sunny look of his would soon repair:
But, too unruly deer, he breaks the pale
And feeds from home: poor I am but his stale.

   Luc. Self-harming jealousy! fie, beat it hence!   110
   Adr. Unfeeling fools can with such wrongs dis-
     pense.

I know his eye doth homage otherwhere;
Or else what lets it but he would be here?
Sister, you know he promised me a chain;   115
Would that alone, alone he would detain,
So he would keep fair quarter with his bed!
I see the jewel best enameled
Will lose his beauty; yet the gold bides still
That others touch, and often touching will,   120
Where gold; and no man that hath a name
By falsehood and corruption doth it shame.
Since that my beauty cannot please his eye,
I'll weep what's left away and weeping die.

   Luc. How many fond fools serve mad jealousy!   125

                          Exeunt.

II. [ii.] Antipholus of Syracuse re-encounters his servant Dromio and chides him for being unresponsive at their last meeting. This Dromio, of course, denies knowledge of any such exchange between them, and his master finally loses his temper and begins to beat him. Dromio is attempting to appease Antipholus with witty conversation when Adriana and Luciana appear. To the mystification of both master and servant, Adriana pleads with Antipholus not to dishonor their marriage and scolds him for refusing to accompany Dromio home to dinner. In a daze, both men finally accompany the women to the house of the Ephesian Antipholus.

[Scene II. A public place.]

Enter Antipholus [of Syracuse].

S. *Ant.* The gold I gave to Dromio is laid up
Safe at the Centaur, and the heedful slave
Is wandered forth in care to seek me out,
By computation and mine host's report.
I could not speak with Dromio since at first   5
I sent him from the mart. See, here he comes.

Enter Dromio of Syracuse.

How now, sir! is your merry humor altered?
As you love strokes, so jest with me again.
You know no Centaur? You received no gold?
Your mistress sent to have me home to dinner?   10
My house was at the Phoenix? Wast thou mad
That thus so madly thou didst answer me?
    S. *Dro.* What answer, sir? When spake I such a
        word?
    S. *Ant.* Even now, even here, not half an hour   15
        since.
    S. *Dro.* I did not see you since you sent me hence,
Home to the Centaur with the gold you gave me.
    S. *Ant.* Villain, thou didst deny the gold's receipt,
And toldst me of a mistress and a dinner;   20
For which, I hope, thou feltst I was displeased.

28. **earnest:** a quibble on **earnest** meaning "token payment to seal a bargain."

32. **jest upon my love:** take advantage of my affection to jest unseasonably.

33. **make a common of my serious hours:** "treat my hours of business as common property in which every man is free to indulge his humor" (C. H. Herford).

39. **Sconce:** Dromio jests upon another meaning: "an earthwork or other part of a fortification system."

40. **And:** an; if.

41. **sconce:** defensive screen.

42–3. **I shall seek my wit in my shoulders:** i.e., because his head will have been beaten to a level with his shoulders.

47–8. **every why hath a wherefore:** a proverbial idea.

S. *Dro.* I am glad to see you in this merry vein:
What means this jest? I pray you, master, tell me.

   S. *Ant.* Yea, dost thou jeer and flout me in the
     teeth?   25
Thinkst thou I jest? Hold, take thou that, and that.

                                  Beats Dromio.

   S. *Dro.* Hold, sir, for God's sake! now your jest is
     earnest!
Upon what bargain do you give it me?

   S. *Ant.* Because that I familiarly sometimes   30
Do use you for my fool and chat with you,
Your sauciness will jest upon my love
And make a common of my serious hours.
When the sun shines let foolish gnats make sport,
But creep in crannies when he hides his beams.   35
If you will jest with me, know my aspect,
And fashion your demeanor to my looks,
Or I will beat this method in your sconce.

   S. *Dro.* Sconce call you it? So you would leave
battering, I had rather have it a head. And you use   40
these blows long, I must get a sconce for my head,
and ensconce it too; or else I shall seek my wit in my
shoulders. But, I pray, sir, why am I beaten?

   S. *Ant.* Dost thou not know?

   S. *Dro.* Nothing, sir, but that I am beaten.   45

   S. *Ant.* Shall I tell you why?

   S. *Dro.* Ay, sir, and wherefore; for they say every
     why hath a wherefore.

51. **urging:** mentioning.

63. **wants that:** lacks what.

64. **In good time:** "very well; I'll indulge you a little longer." Usually the phrase is an ironic exclamation, here indicating Antipholus' effort to be patient.

65. **Basting:** i.e., beating.

S. Ant. Why, first, for flouting me; and then,
  wherefore,   50
For urging it the second time to me.

S. Dro. Was there ever any man thus beaten out of
  season,
When in the why and the wherefore is neither rhyme
  nor reason?   55
Well, sir, I thank you.

S. Ant. Thank me, sir! For what?

S. Dro. Marry, sir, for this something that you
gave me for nothing.

S. Ant. I'll make you amends next, to give you   60
nothing for something. But say, sir, is it dinnertime?

S. Dro. No, sir: I think the meat wants that I have.

S. Ant. In good time, sir; what's that?

S. Dro. Basting.   65

S. Ant. Well, sir, then 'twill be dry.

S. Dro. If it be, sir, I pray you, eat none of it.

S. Ant. Your reason?

S. Dro. Lest it make you choleric and purchase me
another dry basting.   70

S. Ant. Well, sir, learn to jest in good time: there's
a time for all things.

S. Dro. I durst have denied that before you were
so choleric.

S. Ant. By what rule, sir?   75

S. Dro. Marry, sir, by a rule as plain as the bald
pate of Father Time himself.

S. Ant. Let's hear it.

81. **fine and recovery:** legal terminology. A **fine** is an agreement for the transfer of land, a **recovery** a process for property conveyance. Both terms carry an implication of collusive action between the parties involved.

85. **excrement:** outgrowth. The term was applied to both hair and nails.

92. **lose his hair:** i.e., by consorting with prostitutes and contracting venereal disease.

99. **sound:** healthy.

101. **falsing:** doing wrong.

105. **tiring:** attiring; dressing his hair.

S. Dro. There's no time for a man to recover his
hair that grows bald by nature.   80

S. Ant. May he not do it by fine and recovery?

S. Dro. Yes, to pay a fine for a periwig and recover
the lost hair of another man.

S. Ant. Why is Time such a niggard of hair, being,
as it is, so plentiful an excrement?   85

S. Dro. Because it is a blessing that he bestows on
beasts: and what he hath scanted men in hair, he
hath given them in wit.

S. Ant. Why, but there's many a man hath more
hair than wit.   90

S. Dro. Not a man of those but he hath the wit to
lose his hair.

S. Ant. Why, thou didst conclude hairy men plain
dealers without wit.

S. Dro. The plainer dealer, the sooner lost: yet he   95
loseth it in a kind of jollity.

S. Ant. For what reason?

S. Dro. For two, and sound ones too.

S. Ant. Nay, not sound, I pray you.

S. Dro. Sure ones, then.   100

S. Ant. Nay, not sure, in a thing falsing.

S. Dro. Certain ones, then.

S. Ant. Name them.

S. Dro. The one, to save the money that he spends
in tiring; the other, that at dinner they should not   105
drop in his porridge.

S. Ant. You would all this time have proved there
is no time for all things.

117. **wafts:** beckons.
118. **strange:** distant; cold.
119. **aspects:** glances.
134. **fall:** let fall.
135. **gulf:** whirlpool.

Marchantes wife.

A merchant's wife. From Richard Day, *A Book of Christian Prayers* (1590).

S. *Dro.* Marry, and did, sir: namely, no time to
recover hair lost by nature.   110

S. *Ant.* But your reason was not substantial why
there is no time to recover.

S. *Dro.* Thus I mend it: Time himself is bald and
therefore to the world's end will have bald fol-
lowers.   115

S. *Ant.* I knew 'twould be a bald conclusion:
But, soft! who wafts us yonder?

Enter Adriana and Luciana.

Adr. Ay, ay, Antipholus, look strange and frown;
Some other mistress hath thy sweet aspects;
I am not Adriana nor thy wife.   120
The time was once when thou unurged wouldst vow
That never words were music to thine ear,
That never object pleasing in thine eye,
That never touch well welcome to thy hand,
That never meat sweet-savored in thy taste,   125
Unless I spake, or looked, or touched, or carved to
      thee.
How comes it now, my husband, O, how comes it,
That thou art then estranged from thyself?
Thyself I call it, being strange to me,   130
That, undividable, incorporate,
Am better than thy dear self's better part.
Ah, do not tear away thyself from me!
For know, my love, as easy mayst thou fall
A drop of water in the breaking gulf,   135

139. **dearly:** grievously.

145. **the stained skin:** i.e., the brand of a harlot.

149. **possessed with an adulterate blot:** i.e., stained by adultery (that of her husband, as she thinks).

153. **strumpeted:** made a strumpet.

155. **distained:** unstained.

And take unmingled thence that drop again,
Without addition or diminishing,
As take from me thyself and not me too.
How dearly would it touch thee to the quick
Shouldst thou but hear I were licentious,   140
And that this body, consecrate to thee,
By ruffian lust should be contaminate!
Wouldst thou not spit at me and spurn at me,
And hurl the name of husband in my face,
And tear the stained skin off my harlot-brow,   145
And from my false hand cut the wedding ring
And break it with a deep-divorcing vow?
I know thou canst; and therefore see thou do it.
I am possessed with an adulterate blot;
My blood is mingled with the crime of lust: 150
For if we two be one and thou play false,
I do digest the poison of thy flesh,
Being strumpeted by thy contagion.
Keep, then, fair league and truce with thy true bed,
I live distained, thou undishonored.   155
    S. Ant. Plead you to me, fair dame? I know you
      not:
In Ephesus I am but two hours old,
As strange unto your town as to your talk;
Who, every word by all my wit being scanned,   160
Wants wit in all one word to understand.
    Luc. Fie, brother! how the world is changed with
      you!
When were you wont to use my sister thus?
She sent for you by Dromio home to dinner.   165

173. **course and drift:** intention.

184. **Be it my wrong you are from me exempt:** let me suffer the wrong of being denied by you.

189. **communicate:** partake.

190. **from:** away from.

193. **confusion:** ruin.

194. **moves:** mentions.

S. Ant. By Dromio?

S. Dro. By me?

Adr. By thee; and this thou didst return from him,
That he did buffet thee and, in his blows,
Denied my house for his, me for his wife.   170

   S. Ant. Did you converse, sir, with this gentle-
     woman?
What is the course and drift of your compact?

   S. Dro. I, sir? I never saw her till this time.

   S. Ant. Villain, thou liest; for even her very words 175
Didst thou deliver to me on the mart.

   S. Dro. I never spake with her in all my life.

   S. Ant. How can she thus, then, call us by our
     names,
Unless it be by inspiration?   180

   Adr. How ill agrees it with your gravity
To counterfeit thus grossly with your slave,
Abetting him to thwart me in my mood!
Be it my wrong you are from me exempt,
But wrong not that wrong with a more contempt.   185
Come, I will fasten on this sleeve of thine:
Thou art an elm, my husband, I a vine,
Whose weakness, married to thy stronger state,
Makes me with thy strength to communicate.
If aught possess thee from me, it is dross,   190
Usurping ivy, brier, or idle moss,
Who, all for want of pruning, with intrusion
Infect thy sap and live on thy confusion.

   S. Ant. To me she speaks; she moves me for her
     theme: 195

209. **sot:** blockhead.

214. **ape:** imitation (of someone else) and, possibly, "plaything."

216. **grass:** freedom.

224. **shrive:** hear confession and assign penance.

What, was I married to her in my dream?
Or sleep I now and think I hear all this?
What error drives our eyes and ears amiss?
Until I know this sure uncertainty,
I'll entertain the offered fallacy.   200

   Luc. Dromio, go bid the servants spread for
    dinner.
   S. Dro. O, for my beads! I cross me for a sinner.
This is the fairyland: O spite of spites!
We talk with goblins, owls, and sprites: 205
If we obey them not, this will ensue,
They'll suck our breath or pinch us black and blue.
   Luc. Why pratest thou to thyself and answerst not?
Dromio, thou drone, thou snail, thou slug, thou sot!
   S. Dro. I am transformed, master, am I not?   210
   S. Ant. I think thou art in mind, and so am I.
   S. Dro. Nay, master, both in mind and in my shape.
   S. Ant. Thou hast thine own form.
   S. Dro.   No, I am an ape.
   Luc. If thou art changed to aught, 'tis to an ass.   215
   S. Dro. 'Tis true; she rides me, and I long for grass.
'Tis so, I am an ass; else it could never be
But I should know her as well as she knows me.
   Adr. Come, come, no longer will I be a fool,
To put the finger in the eye and weep   220
Whilst man and master laughs my woes to scorn.
Come, sir, to dinner. Dromio, keep the gate.
Husband, I'll dine above with you today
And shrive you of a thousand idle pranks.
Sirrah, if any ask you for your master,   225

229. **well-advised:** sane.

232. **at all adventures:** no matter what the outcome.

Say he dines forth, and let no creature enter.
Come, sister. Dromio, play the porter well.

   S. Ant. Am I in earth, in Heaven, or in hell?
Sleeping or waking? mad or well-advised?
Known unto these and to myself disguised!   230
I'll say as they say and persever so,
And in this mist at all adventures go.

   S. Dro. Master, shall I be porter at the gate?

   Adr. Ay, and let none enter, lest I break your pate.

   Luc. Come, come, Antipholus, we dine too late.   235

                     Exeunt.

THE COMEDY
OF ERRORS

ACT III

III. i. Antipholus of Ephesus approaches his house with Angelo, a goldsmith (from whom he has ordered a chain for his wife), the merchant Balthazar, and his servant Dromio. Dromio of Syracuse responds to Antipholus' call, when he finds his door locked, and refuses to admit them. A servant girl and Adriana both support Dromio in denying them entrance and Antipholus finally departs in a rage, convinced that his wife is entertaining a lover. Balthazar persuades him not to shame his wife publicly, but Antipholus decides that in retaliation for her behavior he will go to dine with a woman of his acquaintance who has already caused Adriana some groundless jealousy. He bids Angelo bring the chain he has ordered to the woman's house, the Porpentine.

ᴵᴵᴵᴵᴵᴵᴵᴵᴵᴵᴵᴵᴵᴵᴵᴵᴵᴵᴵᴵᴵᴵᴵᴵᴵᴵᴵᴵᴵᴵᴵᴵ

5. **carcanet:** necklace (the **chain** mentioned at II. [i]. 115.
7. **face me down:** maintain against my denial.

ACT III

Scene I. [Before the house of Antipholus of Ephesus.]

Enter Antipholus of Ephesus, his man Dromio,
Angelo the goldsmith, and Balthazar the merchant.

E. Ant. Good Signior Angelo, you must excuse us
    all;
My wife is shrewish when I keep not hours.
Say that I lingered with you at your shop
To see the making of her carcanet   5
And that tomorrow you will bring it home.
But here's a villain that would face me down
He met me on the mart, and that I beat him
And charged him with a thousand marks in gold,
And that I did deny my wife and house.   10
Thou drunkard, thou, what didst thou mean by this?
    E. Dro. Say what you will, sir, but I know what I
    know;
That you beat me at the mart, I have your hand to
    show: 15
If the skin were parchment, and the blows you gave
    were ink,
Your own handwriting would tell you what I think.

26

20. **Marry:** "by the Virgin Mary"; truly.
24. **sad:** grave.
26. **answer:** correspond to; accord with.
28–9. **hold your dainties cheap, sir, and your welcome dear:** i.e., value your sincere welcome more than the dainties you may offer.
40. **cates:** dainties.
46. **Mome:** blockhead; **malt-horse:** drudge.
47. **patch:** fool.

E. Ant. I think thou art an ass.

E. Dro. Marry, so it doth appear 20
By the wrongs I suffer and the blows I bear.
I should kick, being kicked; and, being at that pass,
You would keep from my heels and beware of an ass.

E. Ant. Y'are sad, Signior Balthazar: pray God our
cheer 25
May answer my good will and your good welcome
here.

Bal. I hold your dainties cheap, sir, and your
welcome dear.

E. Ant. O, Signior Balthazar, either at flesh or fish, 30
A table full of welcome makes scarce one dainty dish.

Bal. Good meat, sir, is common: that every churl
affords.

E. Ant. And welcome more common; for that's
nothing but words. 35

Bal. Small cheer and great welcome makes a merry
feast.

E. Ant. Ay, to a niggardly host and more sparing
guest:
But though my cates be mean, take them in good 40
part;
Better cheer may you have, but not with better heart.
But, soft! my door is locked. Go bid them let us in.

E. Dro. Maud, Bridget, Marian, Cicely, Gillian,
Ginn! 45

S. Dro. [*Within*] Mome, malt-horse, capon,
coxcomb, idiot, patch!

48–9. **sit down at the hatch:** apparently a colloquialism for "be quiet."

57. **catch cold on's feet:** suffer humiliation; a proverbial phrase.

66. **owe:** own.

73–4. **Thou wouldst have changed thy face for a name, or thy name for an ass:** i.e., you would have wished for yourself a different identity.

75. **coil:** commotion.

Either get thee from the door or sit down at the
    hatch.
Dost thou conjure for wenches, that thou callst for   50
    such store,
When one is one too many? Go get thee from the
    door.

  E. Dro. What patch is made our porter? My
    master stays in the street.   55

  S. Dro. [*Within*] Let him walk from whence he
    came, lest he catch cold on's feet.

  E. Ant. Who talks within there? ho, open the door!

  S. Dro. [*Within*] Right, sir, I'll tell you when, and
    you'll tell me wherefore.   60

  E. Ant. Wherefore? for my dinner: I have not
    dined today.

  S. Dro. [*Within*] Nor today here you must not;
    come again when you may.

  E. Ant. What art thou that keepst me out from the   65
    house I owe?

  S. Dro. [*Within*] The porter for this time, sir, and
    my name is Dromio.

  E. Dro. O villain, thou hast stolen both mine office
    and my name!   70
The one ne'er got me credit, the other mickle blame.
If thou hadst been Dromio today in my place,
Thou wouldst have changed thy face for a name, or
    thy name for an ass.

  Luce. [*Within*] What a coil is there, Dromio! Who   75
    are those at the gate?

  E. Dro. Let my master in, Luce.

84. **When? can you tell?:** a phrase expressing denial or opposition.

87. **minion:** creature.

99–100. **and a pair of stocks:** so long as there is a pair of stocks.

Luce. [*Within*]   Faith, no; he comes too late:
And so tell your master.

E. Dro.   O Lord, I must laugh!   80
Have at you with a proverb. Shall I set in my
    staff?

Luce. [*Within*] Have at you with another: that's,
    When? can you tell?

S. Dro. [*Within*] If thy name be called Luce–Luce,   85
    thou hast answered him well.

E. Ant. Do you hear, you minion? You'll let us in,
    I hope?

Luce. [*Within*] I thought to have asked you.

S. Dro. [*Within*]   And you said no.   90

E. Dro. So, come, help: well struck! there was
    blow for blow.

E. Ant. Thou baggage, let me in.

Luce. [*Within*]   Can you tell for whose sake?

E. Dro. Master, knock the door hard.   95

Luce. [*Within*]   Let him knock till it ache.

E. Ant. You'll cry for this, minion, if I beat the
    door down.

Luce. [*Within*] What needs all that, and a pair of
    stocks in the town?   100

Adr. [*Within*] Who is that at the door that keeps
    all this noise?

S. Dro. [*Within*] By my truth, your town is
    troubled with unruly boys.

E. Ant. Are you there, wife? You might have come   105
    before.

109–10. **If you went in pain, master, this "knave" would go sore:** i.e., because if Antipholus is a "knave" (menial), he and his servant are two of a kind.

113. **part:** depart.

123–24. **bought and sold:** cheated.

133. **breaking:** disciplining.

134. **hind:** base fellow.

Adr. [*Within*] Your wife, sir knave! Go get you
from the door.

E. Dro. If you went in pain, master, this "knave"
would go sore. 110

Ang. Here is neither cheer, sir, nor welcome: we
would fain have either.

Bal. In debating which was best, we shall part with
neither.

E. Dro. They stand at the door, master: bid them 115
welcome hither.

E. Ant. There is something in the wind, that we
cannot get in.

E. Dro. You would say so, master, if your garments
were thin. 120

Your cake here is warm within; you stand here in the
cold.

It would make a man mad as a buck, to be so bought
and sold.

E. Ant. Go fetch me something: I'll break ope the 125
gate.

S. Dro. [*Within*] Break any breaking here, and I'll
break your knave's pate.

E. Dro. A man may break a word with you, sir, and
words are but wind; 130

Ay, and break it in your face, so he break it not behind.

S. Dro. [*Within*] It seems thou wantst breaking:
out upon thee, hind!

E. Dro. Here's too much "out upon thee!" I pray 135
thee, let me in.

139. **crow:** crowbar.

144–45. **pluck a crow together:** settle our differences.

149. **compass of suspect:** reach of suspicion.

151. **Once this:** in short.

155. **made:** shut.

161. **in the stirring passage:** while there is so much activity in the street.

162. **A vulgar comment will be made of it:** it will be noted by everyone. **Comment** means ocular rather than verbal observation here.

163. **rout:** mob.

164. **ungalled estimation:** undamaged reputation.

S. *Dro.* [*Within*] Ay, when fowls have no feathers,
  and fish have no fin.
E. *Ant.* Well, I'll break in: go borrow me a crow.
E. *Dro.* A crow without feather? Master, mean you 140
  so?
For a fish without a fin, there's a fowl without a
  feather:
If a crow help us in, sirrah, we'll pluck a crow
  together.   145
  E. *Ant.* Go, get thee gone; fetch me an iron crow.
  Bal. Have patience, sir.   O, let it not be sol
Herein you war against your reputation,
And draw within the compass of suspect
The unviolated honor of your wife.   150
Once this, your long experience of her wisdom,
Her sober virtue, years, and modesty,
Plead on her part some cause to you unknown;
And doubt not, sir, but she will well excuse
Why at this time the doors are made against you. 155
Be ruled by me: depart in patience,
And let us to the Tiger all to dinner;
And about evening come yourself alone
To know the reason of this strange restraint.
If by strong hand you offer to break in   160
Now, in the stirring passage of the day,
A vulgar comment will be made of it
And that supposed by the common rout
Against your yet ungalled estimation
That may with foul intrusion enter in   165
And dwell upon your grave when you are dead;

167. **lives upon succession:** is self-perpetuating.

170. **in despite of mirth:** despite my indisposition to mirth.

178. **Porpentine:** Porcupine.

182. **entertain:** receive; welcome.

<hr>

III. [ii.] Antipholus of Syracuse has fallen in love with Luciana, who tries to point out to him his duty to his supposed wife, her sister. When he continues to protest his love, she goes to summon Adriana. As she departs, Dromio comes running in and seeks reassurance of his identity from his master. A kitchenmaid, whom Dromio describes in uncomplimentary terms, has greeted him as her husband. Antipholus has had enough and orders Dromio to engage passage for them on any ship leaving Ephesus that very night. He is convinced that the city, which is renowned for sorcery, is full of nothing but witches, and he does not exempt Luciana, who has enchanted him. In the meantime, Angelo appears with the chain that Antipholus of Ephesus ordered from him. When Angelo leaves the chain with him, expecting to collect his payment at suppertime, Antipholus wonders, but he is disposed to accept freely offered gifts.

For slander lives upon succession,
Forever housed where it gets possession.

  E. Ant. You have prevailed; I will depart in quiet,
And, in despite of mirth, mean to be merry.   170
I know a wench of excellent discourse,
Pretty and witty; wild, and yet, too, gentle:
There will we dine. This woman that I mean
My wife—but, I protest, without desert—
Hath oftentimes upbraided me withal: 175
To her will we to dinner. [*To Angelo*] Get you home
And fetch the chain; by this I know 'tis made.
Bring it, I pray you, to the Porpentine,
For there's the house. That chain will I bestow—
Be it for nothing but to spite my wife—   180
Upon mine hostess there: good sir, make haste.
Since mine own doors refuse to entertain me,
I'll knock elsewhere, to see if they'll disdain me.

  Ang. I'll meet you at that place some hour hence.

  E. Ant. Do so. This jest shall cost me some expense. 185
                                        Exeunt.

[Scene II. Before the house of Antipholus of
Ephesus.]

Enter Luciana, with Antipholus of Syracuse.

  Luc. And may it be that you have quite forgot
A husband's office? Shall, Antipholus,
Even in the spring of love, thy love-springs rot?

12. **become disloyalty:** give disloyalty a fair appearance.

13. **like virtue's harbinger:** i.e., in garments proclaiming it the servant of virtue.

15. **carriage:** behavior.

17. **attaint:** disgrace.

20. **bastard:** spurious.

23. **compact of credit:** completely credulous.

25. **in your motion turn:** revolve around you.

28. **vain:** worldly.

32. **hit of:** guess.

Shall love, in building, grow so ruinous?
If you did wed my sister for her wealth,   5
Then for her wealth's sake use her with more kind-
     ness;
Or, if you like elsewhere, do it by stealth:
Muffle your false love with some show of blindness.
Let not my sister read it in your eye;   10
Be not thy tongue thy own shame's orator;
Look sweet, speak fair, become disloyalty;
Apparel vice like virtue's harbinger;
Bear a fair presence, though your heart be tainted;
Teach sin the carriage of a holy saint;   15
Be secret-false: what need she be acquainted?
What simple thief brags of his own attaint?
'Tis double wrong to truant with your bed
And let her read it in thy looks at board.
Shame hath a bastard fame, well managed;   20
Ill deeds is doubled with an evil word.
Alas, poor women! make us but believe,
Being compact of credit, that you love us;
Though others have the arm, show us the sleeve:
We in your motion turn, and you may move us.   25
Then, gentle brother, get you in again;
Comfort my sister, cheer her, call her wife:
'Tis holy sport to be a little vain
When the sweet breath of flattery conquers strife.
   S. Ant. Sweet mistress—what your name is else, I   30
     know not,
Nor by what wonder you do hit of mine—
Less in your knowledge and your grace you show not

36. **earthy-gross conceit:** dull imagination of a mortal.

38. **folded:** concealed.

46. **decline:** incline.

47. **train:** entice.

54. **light:** (1) wanton; (2) light in weight.

56. **mated:** (1) overcome with confusion; bested; (2) wedded.

Ulysses listening to the sirens. From Geoffrey Whitney, *A Choice of Emblems* (1586).

Than our earth's wonder, more than earth divine.
Teach me, dear creature, how to think and speak;   35
Lay open to my earthy-gross conceit,
Smothered in errors, feeble, shallow, weak,
The folded meaning of your words' deceit.
Against my soul's pure truth why labor you
To make it wander in an unknown field?   40
Are you a god? Would you create me new?
Transform me, then, and to your power I'll yield.
But if that I am I, then well I know
Your weeping sister is no wife of mine,
Nor to her bed no homage do I owe: 45
Far more, far more to you do I decline.
O, train me not, sweet mermaid, with thy note,
To drown me in thy sister's flood of tears:
Sing, siren, for thyself, and I will dote:
Spread o'er the silver waves thy golden hairs,   50
And as a bed I'll take them and there lie;
And, in that glorious supposition, think
He gains by death that hath such means to die:
Let Love, being light, be drowned if she sink!
 Luc. What, are you mad, that you do reason so?   55
 S. Ant. Not mad, but mated: how, I do not know.
 Luc. It is a fault that springeth from your eye.
 S. Ant. For gazing on your beams, fair sun, being
  by.
 Luc. Gaze where you should and that will clear   60
  your sight.
 S. Ant. As good to wink, sweet love, as look on
  night.

71. **Heaven's claim:** claim to Heaven; hope of salvation.

Luc. Why call you me "love"? Call my sister so.

S. Ant. Thy sister's sister.   65

Luc.   That's my sister.

S. Ant.   No!
It is thyself, mine own self's better part,
Mine eye's clear eye, my dear heart's dearer heart,
My food, my fortune, and my sweet hope's aim,   70
My sole earth's Heaven and my Heaven's claim.

Luc. All this my sister is, or else should be.

S. Ant. Call thyself sister, sweet, for I am thee.
Thee will I love and with thee lead my life:
Thou hast no husband yet, nor I no wife.   75
Give me thy hand.

Luc.   O, soft, sir! hold you still:
I'll fetch my sister, to get her good will.   *Exit.*

Enter Dromio of Syracuse.

S. Ant. Why, how now, Dromio! where runnest
thou so fast?   80

S. Dro. Do you know me, sir? Am I Dromio? Am I
your man? Am I myself?

S. Ant. Thou art Dromio, thou art my man, thou art
thyself.

S. Dro. I am an ass, I am a woman's man and be- 85
sides myself.

S. Ant. What woman's man? and how besides thyself?

S. Dro. Marry, sir, besides myself, I am due to a

99. **sir-reverence:** save your reverence (an apology for being presumptuous or mentioning something offensive).

114. **in grain:** i.e., dyed in grain (Scarlet Grain); thus, permanent.

woman, one that claims me, one that haunts me, one   90
that will have me.

S. Ant. What claim lays she to thee?

S. Dro. Marry, sir, such claim as you would lay to
your horse; and she would have me as a beast: not
that, I being a beast she would have me; but that she,   95
being a very beastly creature, lays claim to me.

S. Ant. What is she?

S. Dro. A very reverent body: ay, such a one as a
man may not speak of without he say "sir-reverence."
I have but lean luck in the match, and yet is she a   100
wondrous fat marriage.

S. Ant. How dost thou mean a fat marriage?

S. Dro. Marry, sir, she's the kitchen wench and all
grease; and I know not what use to put her to but to
make a lamp of her and run from her by her own light.   105
I warrant, her rags, and the tallow in them, will burn
a Poland winter. If she lives till Doomsday, she'll burn
a week longer than the whole world.

S. Ant. What complexion is she of?

S. Dro. Swart, like my shoe, but her face nothing   110
like so clean kept; for why? She sweats: a man may
go over shoes in the grime of it.

S. Ant. That's a fault that water will mend.

S. Dro. No, sir, 'tis in grain: Noah's flood could not
do it.   115

S. Ant. What's her name?

S. Dro. Nell, sir; but her name and three quarters,
that's an ell and three quarters, will not measure her
from hip to hip.

131–32. **armed and reverted, making war against her heir:** in armed rebellion, a reference to the civil wars in France, the **heir** being Henry of Navarre. The pun on hair/heir also suggests loss of hair from venereal (French) disease.

134. **chalky cliffs:** i.e., teeth.

136. **salt rheum:** watery discharge from eyes or nose.

143–44. **declining their rich aspect to the hot breath of Spain:** possibly, curving toward the mouth; hooked.

145. **carracks:** merchant ships; **ballast:** loaded.

146. **the Netherlands:** a euphemism for "private parts."

148. **drudge, or diviner:** although she seems to be a kitchen drudge, her knowledge of him suggests the power of divination.

149. **assured:** pledged.

S. Ant. Then she bears some breadth?   120

S. Dro. No longer from head to foot than from hip
to hip: she is spherical, like a globe. I could find out
countries in her.

S. Ant. In what part of her body stands Ireland?

S. Dro. Marry, sir, in her buttocks: I found it out   125
by the bogs.

S. Ant. Where Scotland?

S. Dro. I found it by the barrenness: hard in the
palm of the hand.

S. Ant. Where France?   130

S. Dro. In her forehead, armed and reverted, making war against her heir.

S. Ant. Where England?

S. Dro. I looked for the chalky cliffs, but I could
find no whiteness in them; but I guess it stood in her   135
chin, by the salt rheum that ran between France and
it.

S. Ant. Where Spain?

S. Dro. Faith, I saw it not, but I felt it hot in her
breath.   140

S. Ant. Where America, the Indies?

S. Dro. O sir, upon her nose, all o'er embellished
with rubies, carbuncles, sapphires, declining their rich
aspect to the hot breath of Spain, who sent whole
armadoes of carracks to be ballast at her nose.   145

S. Ant. Where stood Belgia, the Netherlands?

S. Dro. O sir, I did not look so low. To conclude,
this drudge, or diviner, laid claim to me; called me
Dromio; swore I was assured to her; told me what

155. **curtal:** dock-tailed.

156. **turn i' the wheel:** i.e., like a dog used to turn a spit over the fire.

157. **post:** hasten; **road:** harbor.

privy marks I had about me, as, the mark of my shoul-   150
der, the mole in my neck, the great wart on my left
arm, that I, amazed, ran from her as a witch:
And, I think, if my breast had not been made of faith
    and my heart of steel,
She had transformed me to a curtal dog and made me   155
    turn i' the wheel.

   S. Ant. Go hie thee presently, post to the road.
And if the wind blow any way from shore,
I will not harbor in this town tonight.
If any bark put forth, come to the mart,   160
Where I will walk till thou return to me.
If everyone knows us, and we know none,
'Tis time, I think, to trudge, pack, and be gone.

   S. Dro. As from a bear a man would run for life,
So fly I from her that would be my wife.   *Exit.*   165

   S. Ant. There's none but witches do inhabit here;
And therefore 'tis high time that I were hence.
She that doth call me husband even my soul
Doth for a wife abhor. But her fair sister,
Possessed with such a gentle, sovereign grace,   170
Of such enchanting presence and discourse,
Hath almost made me traitor to myself:
But, lest myself be guilty to self-wrong,
I'll stop mine ears against the mermaid's song.

       Enter Angelo with the chain.

   Ang. Master Antipholus.   175
   S. Ant.   Ay, that's my name.

183. **bespoke:** ordered.
187. **soon:** this evening.
193. **vain:** foolish.

   Ang. I know it well, sir: lo, here is the chain.
I thought to have ta'en you at the Porpentine:
The chain unfinished made me stay thus long.
   S. Ant. What is your will that I shall do with this?   180
   Ang. What please yourself, sir: I have made it for
     you.
   S. Ant. Made it for me, sir! I bespoke it not.
   Ang. Not once, nor twice, but twenty times you
     have.   185
Go home with it and please your wife withal,
And soon at suppertime I'll visit you
And then receive my money for the chain.
   S. Ant. I pray you, sir, receive the money now,
For fear you ne'er see chain nor money more.   190
   Ang. You are a merry man, sir: fare you well. *Exit.*
   S. Ant. What I should think of this I cannot tell,
But this I think: there's no man is so vain
That would refuse so fair an offered chain.
I see a man here needs not live by shifts,   195
When in the streets he meets such golden gifts.
I'll to the mart and there for Dromio stay:
If any ship put out, then straight away.
                            Exit.

THE COMEDY
OF ERRORS

ACT IV

IV. i. Angelo is pressed for payment by a merchant to whom he owes a sum exactly equal to the price of the chain he made for Antipholus of Ephesus. The latter appears with Dromio, whom he sends to buy a rope with which to beat his wife and her friends. He then turns to Angelo and complains of his failure to deliver the chain as promised. Angelo protests that he has delivered it and requests payment to satisfy his creditor and, threatened with arrest if he does not pay the merchant, he charges an officer to arrest Antipholus if he will not pay for the chain. In the midst of this confusion, Dromio of Syracuse enters and announces to Antipholus that he has engaged passage in a bark for Epidamnum, which only awaits their embarkation before sailing. Antipholus denies knowledge of any ship and asks for the rope which he sent the other Dromio to buy. But the present emergency allowing no time for prolonged argument, he sends Dromio to Adriana for the sum necessary to gain his release from custody.

6. **attach:** arrest.
8. **growing:** coming due.
12. **Pleaseth you:** if it please you to.

ACT IV

Scene I. [A public place.]

Enter [Second] Merchant, [Angelo], the goldsmith,
and an Officer.

2nd. Mer. You know since Pentecost the sum is due,
And since I have not much importuned you;
Nor now I had not but that I am bound
To Persia and want guilders for my voyage:
Therefore make present satisfaction,   5
Or I'll attach you by this officer.
    Ang. Even just the sum that I do owe to you
Is growing to me by Antipholus,
And in the instant that I met with you
He had of me a chain: at five o'clock   10
I shall receive the money for the same.
Pleaseth you walk with me down to his house,
I will discharge my bond and thank you too.

Enter Antipholus of Ephesus and Dromio [of
Ephesus] from the Courtesan's.

Off. That labor may you save: see where he comes.

21-2. **I buy a thousand pound a year: I buy a rope:** possibly, "Will I buy a rope? As gladly as I would accept a thousand pounds a year of income."

23. **holp:** helped; supported.

26. **Belike:** perhaps.

28. **Saving your merry humor:** i.e., no offense if I am not in the same merry humor.

30. **chargeful:** expensive.

33. **presently discharged:** immediately satisfied.

E. Ant. While I go to the goldsmith's house, go thou 15
And buy a rope's end: that will I bestow
Among my wife and her confederates,
For locking me out of my doors by day.
But, soft! I see the goldsmith. Get thee gone;
Buy thou a rope and bring it home to me. 20

E. Dro. I buy a thousand pound a year: I buy a
rope! *Exit.*

E. Ant. A man is well holp up that trusts to you:
I promised your presence and the chain;
But neither chain nor goldsmith came to me. 25
Belike you thought our love would last too long,
If it were chained together, and therefore came not.

Ang. Saving your merry humor, here's the note
How much your chain weighs to the utmost carat,
The fineness of the gold and chargeful fashion, 30
Which doth amount to three odd ducats more
Than I stand debted to this gentleman.
I pray you, see him presently discharged,
For he is bound to sea and stays but for it.

E. Ant. I am not furnished with the present money; 35
Besides, I have some business in the town.
Good signior, take the stranger to my house,
And with you take the chain and bid my wife
Disburse the sum on the receipt thereof:
Perchance I will be there as soon as you. 40

Ang. Then you will bring the chain to her yourself?

E. Ant. No, bear it with you, lest I come not time
enough.

50. **to blame:** too much to blame.

62. **send me by some token:** send me with a note authorizing your wife to give me the money.

65. **brook:** endure.

66. **whe'er:** whether; **answer:** pay.

Ang. Well, sir, I will. Have you the chain about
   you?   45

E. Ant. And if I have not, sir, I hope you have;
Or else you may return without your money.

Ang. Nay, come, I pray you, sir, give me the chain:
Both wind and tide stays for this gentleman,
And I, to blame, have held him here too long.   50

E. Ant. Good Lord! you use this dalliance to excuse
Your breach of promise to the Porpentine.
I should have chid you for not bringing it,
But, like a shrew, you first begin to brawl.

2nd. Mer. The hour steals on: I pray you, sir, dis-   55
   patch.

Ang. You hear how he importunes me—the chain!

E. Ant. Why, give it to my wife and fetch your
   money.

Ang. Come, come, you know I gave it you even   60
   now.
Either send the chain, or send me by some token.

E. Ant. Fie, now you run this humor out of breath.
Come, where's the chain? I pray you, let me see it.

2nd. Mer. My business cannot brook this dalliance.   65
Good sir, say whe'er you'll answer me or no:
If not, I'll leave him to the officer.

E. Ant. I answer you! What should I answer you?

Ang. The money that you owe me for the chain.

E. Ant. I owe you none till I receive the chain.   70

Ang. You know I gave it you half an hour since.

E. Ant. You gave me none; you wrong me much to
   say so.

75. **stands upon:** affects.

86. **apparently:** obviously.

95. **fraughtage:** cargo; baggage.

98. **is in her trim:** has her sails trimmed to put forth.

A merchant vessel. From Henry Peacham, *Minerva Britanna* (1612).

Ang. You wrong me more, sir, in denying it;
Consider how it stands upon my credit.   75
2nd. Mer. Well, officer, arrest him at my suit.
Off. I do, and charge you in the Duke's name to
obey me.
Ang. This touches me in reputation.
Either consent to pay this sum for me,   80
Or I attach you by this officer.
E. Ant. Consent to pay thee that I never had!
Arrest me, foolish fellow, if thou darest.
Ang. Here is thy fee: arrest him, officer.
I would not spare my brother in this case,   85
If he should scorn me so apparently.
Off. I do arrest you, sir: you hear the suit.
E. Ant. I do obey thee till I give thee bail.
But, sirrah, you shall buy this sport as dear
As all the metal in your shop will answer.   90
Ang. Sir, sir, I shall have law in Ephesus,
To your notorious shame, I doubt it not.

Enter Dromio of Syracuse, from the Bay.

S. Dro. Master, there is a bark of Epidamnum
That stays but till her owner comes aboard,
And then she bears away. Our fraughtage, sir,   95
I have conveyed aboard; and I have bought
The oil, the balsamum, and aqua vitae.
The ship is in her trim; the merry wind
Blows fair from land: they stay for nought at all
But for their owner, master, and yourself.   100

101. **peevish:** silly.

104. **waftage:** sea passage.

107. **rope's end:** thrashing.

119. **Dowsabel:** literally, equivalent to "sweet-heart," used sarcastically.

120. **compass:** (1) embrace; (2) achieve (as a wife).

E. Ant. How now! a madman! Why, thou peevish
   sheep,
What ship of Epidamnum stays for me?

S. Dro. A ship you sent me to, to hire waftage.

E. Ant. Thou drunken slave, I sent thee for a rope, 105
And told thee to what purpose and what end.

S. Dro. You sent me for a rope's end as soon:
You sent me to the Bay, sir, for a bark.

E. Ant. I will debate this matter at more leisure
And teach your ears to list me with more heed. 110
To Adriana, villain, hie thee straight:
Give her this key and tell her, in the desk
That's covered o'er with Turkish tapestry
There is a purse of ducats: let her send it.
Tell her I am arrested in the street 115
And that shall bail me. Hie thee, slave, be gone!
On, officer, to prison till it come.

                         Exeunt [all but Dromio].

S. Dro. To Adriana! That is where we dined,
Where Dowsabel did claim me for her husband:
She is too big, I hope, for me to compass. 120
Thither I must, although against my will,
For servants must their masters' minds fulfil.

                                Exit.

IV. [ii.] Luciana has reported Antipholus' love-making to Adriana, who is saddened by this evidence of her husband's disloyalty. Dromio of Syracuse hastily enters and reports his master's arrest and his need for a sum to satisfy the goldsmith for the chain. Adriana promptly supplies the money and bids Dromio bring Antipholus home at once.

||||||||||||||||||||||||||||||||||||||

2. **austerely in his eye:** i.e., by the austerity of his expression.

6. **his heart's meteors tilting in his face:** i.e., conflicting expressions betraying his emotions.

7. **no right:** the negative adds emphasis to the denial.

8. **spite:** resentment.

10. **true he swore:** he swore truly in that he has so neglected his wife that she rarely sees him.

21. **his:** its.

25. **Stigmatical in making:** deformed of body.

[Scene II. The house of Antipholus of Ephesus.]

Enter Adriana and Luciana.

Adr. Ah, Luciana, did he tempt thee so?
Mightst thou perceive austerely in his eye
That he did plead in earnest? yea or no?
Looked he or red or pale, or sad or merrily?
What observation madest thou, in this case,   5
Of his heart's meteors tilting in his face?
  Luc. First he denied you had in him no right.
  Adr. He meant he did me none: the more my spite.
  Luc. Then swore he that he was a stranger here.
  Adr. And true he swore, though yet forsworn he   10
    were.
  Luc. Then pleaded I for you.
  Adr.   And what said he?
  Luc. That love I begged for you he begged of me.
  Adr. With what persuasion did he tempt thy love?   15
  Luc. With words that in an honest suit might move:
First he did praise my beauty, then my speech.
  Adr. Didst speak him fair?
  Luc.   Have patience, I beseech.
  Adr. I cannot, nor I will not, hold me still: 20
My tongue, though not my heart, shall have his will.
He is deformed, crooked, old, and sere,
Ill-faced, worse bodied, shapeless everywhere;
Vicious, ungentle, foolish, blunt, unkind,
Stigmatical in making, worse in mind.   25

32. **Sweet now:** if you'll be so sweet now (addressing himself facetiously).

38. **everlasting:** (1) eternal; (2) durable fabric (used for the dress of police officers in this period).

41. **buff:** a leather used for the clothing of officers.

42. **backfriend:** enemy (and one who creeps up behind one's back); **shoulder-clapper:** term for an arresting official.

42–4. **countermands/The passages of alleys:** prohibits access to narrow alleys; polices the streets.

45–6. **counter:** away from the quarry's scent; i.e., treacherously. The word, like **countermands,** suggests the Counter, a London debtors' prison; **draws dryfoot well:** tracks the quarry by the mere scent of its foot.

48. **hell:** a debtors' prison.

Luc. Who would be jealous, then, of such a one?
No evil lost is wailed when it is gone.

Adr. Ah, but I think him better than I say,
And yet would herein others' eyes were worse.
Far from her nest the lapwing cries away: 30
My heart prays for him, though my tongue do curse.

Enter Dromio of Syracuse.

S. Dro. Here! go: the desk, the purse! Sweet now,
    make haste.
Luc. How hast thou lost thy breath?
S. Dro.   By running fast.   35
Adr. Where is thy master, Dromio? Is he well?
S. Dro. No, he's in Tartar limbo, worse than hell.
A devil in an everlasting garment hath him;
One whose hard heart is buttoned up with steel;
A fiend, a fury, pitiless and rough;   40
A wolf, nay, worse, a fellow all in buff;
A backfriend, a shoulder-clapper, one that counter-
    mands
The passages of alleys, creeks, and narrow lands;
A hound that runs counter and yet draws dryfoot   45
    well;
One that, before the Judgment, carries poor souls to
    hell.
Adr. Why, man, what is the matter?
S. Dro. I do not know the matter: he is 'rested on   50
    the case.
Adr. What, is he arrested? Tell me at whose suit.

60. **band:** bond.
61. **band:** pun on "neckband, collar."
68. **'a:** he.
70. **fondly:** foolishly.
72. **very:** downright.
73. **season:** opportunity.

S. *Dro.* I know not at whose suit he is arrested well;
But is in a suit of buff which 'rested him, that can I
    tell.   55
Will you send him, mistress, redemption, the money
    in his desk?

Adr. Go fetch it, sister. This I wonder at,
                        Exit Luciana.
That he, unknown to me, should be in debt.
Tell me, was he arrested on a band?   60

S. *Dro.* Not on a band, but on a stronger thing:
A chain, a chain! Do you not hear it ring?

Adr. What, the chain?

S. *Dro.* No, no, the bell: 'tis time that I were gone:
It was two ere I left him, and now the clock strikes   65
    one.

Adr. The hours come back! that did I never hear.

S. *Dro.* O, yes, if any hour meet a sergeant, 'a turns
    back for very fear.

Adr. As if Time were in debt! How fondly dost thou   70
    reason!

S. *Dro.* Time is a very bankrupt and owes more
    than he's worth to season.
Nay, he's a thief too: have you not heard men say
That Time comes stealing on by night and day?   75
If Time be in debt and theft, and a sergeant in the
    way,
Hath he not reason to turn back an hour in a day?

       Enter Luciana with a purse.

82. **conceit:** imagination.

||||||||||||||||||||||||||||||||||||||||||||||||||||||||||||||||||||||||||||||||||||||

IV. [iii.] Antipholus of Syracuse wonders at being familiarly greeted by so many in Ephesus and is concluding that the town is full of sorcerers when Dromio encounters him and offers the money for his discharge. Antipholus, of course, does not know what Dromio is talking about and asks him about the ship for their departure. Dromio's reply, that he has already reported on the bark for Epidamnum, confirms Antipholus' conviction that they are all enchanted. The Ephesian Antipholus' courtesan-companion appears and indicates that the chain he holds is the one he had promised her in exchange for a diamond ring she gave him at dinner. He considers her to be a demon or a witch, and he and Dromio depart hastily, leaving the courtesan with the impression that Antipholus is mad. She decides to tell his wife that he has taken her ring forcibly in a fit of madness.

||||||||||||||||||||||||||||||||||||||||||||||

4. **tender:** offer.

10. **imaginary wiles:** tricks of the mind.

11. **Lapland sorcerers:** Lapland, in common with other northern countries, was considered a center of witchcraft and sorcery.

13–4. **have you got the picture of old Adam new appareled: old Adam** is equivalent to human sin. Not seeing the officer, Dromio asks whether Antipholus has succeeded in clothing the nakedness of his offense to gain his release.

Adr. Go, Dromio; there's the money, bear it
    straight;   80
And bring thy master home immediately.
Come, sister: I am pressed down with conceit—
Conceit, my comfort and my injury.

Exeunt.

[Scene III. A public place.]

Enter Antipholus of Syracuse.

S. Ant. There's not a man I meet but doth salute me
As if I were their well-acquainted friend;
And every one doth call me by my name.
Some tender money to me; some invite me;
Some other give me thanks for kindnesses;   5
Some offer me commodities to buy.
Even now a tailor called me in his shop
And showed me silks that he had bought for me,
And therewithal took measure of my body.
Sure, these are but imaginary wiles,   10
And Lapland sorcerers inhabit here.

Enter Dromio of Syracuse.

S. Dro. Master, here's the gold you sent me for.
What, have you got the picture of old Adam new appareled?

25. **sob:** (1) moment's rest; (2) occasion for tears.

26. **decayed:** impoverished.

27. **durance:** (1) imprisonment; (2) stout fabric; **sets up his rest:** is determined.

31. **band:** bond of contract.

39. **hoy:** a small coasting vessel; **angels:** gold coins, with a pun.

A witch of the North exercising her art. From Olaus Magnus, *Historia de gentibus septentrionalibus* (1555).

S. Ant. What gold is this? What Adam dost thou   15
mean?

S. Dro. Not that Adam that kept the Paradise, but
that Adam that keeps the prison. He that goes in the
calf's skin that was killed for the Prodigal; he that
came behind you, sir, like an evil angel, and bid you   20
forsake your liberty.

S. Ant. I understand thee not.

S. Dro. No? Why, 'tis a plain case: he that went,
like a bass viol, in a case of leather; the man, sir, that,
when gentlemen are tired, gives them a sob and 'rests   25
them; he, sir, that takes pity on decayed men and
gives them suits of durance; he that sets up his rest to
do more exploits with his mace than a morris-pike.

S. Ant. What, thou meanst an officer?

S. Dro. Ay, sir, the sergeant of the band; he that   30
brings any man to answer it that breaks his band; one
that thinks a man always going to bed and says, "God
give you good rest!"

S. Ant. Well, sir, there rest in your foolery. Is there
any ship puts forth tonight? May we be gone?   35

S. Dro. Why, sir, I brought you word an hour since
that the bark "Expedition" put forth tonight; and then
were you hindered by the sergeant, to tarry for the
hoy "Delay." Here are the angels that you sent for to
deliver you.   40

S. Ant. The fellow is distract, and so am I;
And here we wander in illusions.
Some blessed power deliver us from hence!

47. **avoid:** be gone.

51. **light:** wanton.

56. **burn:** cause venereal disease.

58. **mend:** supply the lack of; i.e., dine.

62–3. **he must have a long spoon that must eat with the Devil:** proverbial.

PROSTITVIT VETVL9 NVMMOSIOR AERE IVVENCAM

A courtesan. From Theodor de Bry, *Proscenium vitae humanae, sive Emblemata* (1627).

Enter a Courtesan.

Cour. Well met, well met, Master Antipholus.
I see, sir, you have found the goldsmith now.   45
Is that the chain you promised me today?

   S. Ant. Satan, avoid! I charge thee, tempt me not.

   S. Dro. Master, is this Mistress Satan?

   S. Ant. It is the Devil.

   S. Dro. Nay, she is worse, she is the Devil's dam,   50
and here she comes in the habit of a light wench; and
thereof comes that the wenches say, "God damn me":
that's as much to say, "God make me a light wench."
It is written, they appear to men like angels of light.
Light is an effect of fire, and fire will burn; ergo, light   55
wenches will burn. Come not near her.

   Cour. Your man and you are marvelous merry, sir.
Will you go with me? We'll mend our dinner here?

   S. Dro. Master, if you do, expect spoon-meat; or bespeak a long spoon.   60

   S. Ant. Why, Dromio?

   S. Dro. Marry, he must have a long spoon that must
eat with the Devil.

   S. Ant. Avoid then, fiend! What tellst thou me of
     supping?   65
Thou art, as you are all, a sorceress.
I conjure thee to leave me and be gone.

   Cour. Give me the ring of mine you had at dinner,
Or, for my diamond, the chain you promised,
And I'll be gone, sir, and not trouble you.   70

76. **and if:** if.

82. **"Fly pride," says the peacock:** the peacock is a symbol of pride. Dromio puns on another sense of the word: "lust."

85. **demean:** behave (with no connotation of baseness).

94. **way:** admittance.

GLORIA TOTIVS RES EST VANISSIMA MVNDI

The personification of Pride. From Theodor de Bry, *Proscenium vitae humanae, sive Emblemata* (1627).

S. Dro. Some devils ask but the parings of one's
    nail,
A rush, a hair, a drop of blood, a pin,
A nut, a cherry stone;
But she, more covetous, would have a chain.   75
Master, be wise: and if you give it her,
The Devil will shake her chain and fright us with it.
    Cour. I pray you, sir, my ring, or else the chain;
I hope you do not mean to cheat me so.
    S. Ant. Avaunt, thou witch! Come, Dromio, let us 80
    go.
    S. Dro. "Fly pride," says the peacock: mistress, that
    you know.
        Exeunt [*Antipholus of Syracuse and Dromio of
                             Syracuse*].
    Cour. Now, out of doubt Antipholus is mad,
Else would he never so demean himself.   85
A ring he hath of mine worth forty ducats,
And for the same he promised me a chain;
Both one and other he denies me now.
The reason that I gather he is mad,
Besides this present instance of his rage,   90
Is a mad tale he told today at dinner,
Of his own doors being shut against his entrance.
Belike his wife, acquainted with his fits,
On purpose shut the doors against his way.
My way is now to hie home to his house   95
And tell his wife that, being lunatic,
He rushed into my house and took perforce

IV. [iv.] Antipholus of Ephesus, awaiting Dromio's return with the money for his release, is found instead by the other Dromio with the rope. He is beating Dromio in exasperation when Adriana appears with the courtesan and a schoolmaster who claims some knowledge of sorcery. Antipholus' angry behavior is convincing evidence that he is mad or bewitched, and Pinch, the schoolmaster, makes a puny effort to exorcise the demon. Further conversation about the day's events strengthens the impression that Antipholus is dangerous, and Pinch summons help. Although the officer protests, Antipholus and Dromio are bound and dragged away. Immediately afterward Antipholus of Syracuse and the other Dromio enter with swords drawn, and the two women and the officer flee, thinking that the dangerous madman has escaped. The two men from Syracuse think they have routed a pack of witches and can hardly wait to get safely aboard the ship for Epidamnum.

▓▓▓▓▓▓▓▓▓▓▓▓▓▓▓▓▓▓▓▓▓▓

6. **attached:** arrested.
15. **at the rate:** i.e., one rope per ducat.

My ring away. This course I fittest choose,
For forty ducats is too much to lose.

Exit.

[Scene IV. A street.]

Enter Antipholus of Ephesus with the Officer.

E. Ant. Fear me not, man; I will not break away:
I'll give thee, ere I leave thee, so much money
To warrant thee as I am 'rested for.
My wife is in a wayward mood today
And will not lightly trust the messenger.   5
That I should be attached in Ephesus,
I tell you, 'twill sound harshly in her ears.

Enter Dromio of Ephesus with a rope's end.

Here comes my man; I think he brings the money.
How now, sir! have you that I sent you for?
    E. Dro. Here's that, I warrant you, will pay them   10
    all.
    E. Ant. But where's the money?
    E. Dro. Why, sir, I gave the money for the rope.
    E. Ant. Five hundred ducats, villain, for a rope?
    E. Dro. I'll serve you, sir, five hundred at the rate. 15
    E. Ant. To what end did I bid thee hie thee home?
    E. Dro. To a rope's end, sir; and to that end am I
returned.

23. **Good now:** if you will be so good now; please.

25. **whoreson:** good-for-nothing.

28. **sensible:** (1) intelligent; (2) sensitive.

38. **wont:** habitually does.

42. **respect:** be mindful of.

E. Ant. And to that end, sir, I will welcome you.
                              Beating him.

Off. Good sir, be patient.   20

E. Dro. Nay, 'tis for me to be patient: I am in adversity.

Off. Good now, hold thy tongue.

E. Dro. Nay, rather persuade him to hold his hands.

E. Ant. Thou whoreson, senseless villain!   25

E. Dro. I would I were senseless, sir, that I might not feel your blows.

E. Ant. Thou art sensible in nothing but blows, and so is an ass.

E. Dro. I am an ass, indeed; you may prove it by   30
my long ears. I have served him from the hour of my
nativity to this instant and have nothing at his hands
for my service but blows. When I am cold, he heats
me with beating; when I am warm, he cools me with
beating. I am waked with it when I sleep, raised with 35
it when I sit, driven out of doors with it when I go
from home, welcomed home with it when I return:
nay, I bear it on my shoulders as a beggar wont her
brat; and, I think, when he hath lamed me, I shall beg
with it from door to door.   40

E. Ant. Come, go along; my wife is coming yonder.

*Enter Adriana, Luciana, the Courtesan, and a School-
master called Pinch.*

E. Dro. Mistress, *respice finem*, respect your end;

43–4. "beware the rope's end": in Latin, *respice funem*.

52. ecstasy: mad fit.

62. minion: paramour; hussy.

63. companion: base fellow; **saffron:** yellow. The schoolmaster's name, "Pinch," describes his thin face and the adjective **saffron** his sallow complexion.

70. slanders: disgraces.

or rather, the prophecy like the parrot, "beware the
rope's end."

   E. Ant. Wilt thou still talk?   *Beats Dromio.* 45
   Cour. How say you now? Is not your husband mad?
   Adr. His incivility confirms no less.
Good Doctor Pinch, you are a conjurer:
Establish him in his true sense again,
And I will please you what you will demand.   50
   Luc. Alas, how fiery and how sharp he looks!
   Cour. Mark how he trembles in his ecstasy!
   Pinch. Give me your hand and let me feel your
pulse.
   E. Ant. There is my hand and let it feel your ear. 55
                        [Striking him.]
   Pinch. I charge thee, Satan, housed within this man,
To yield possession to my holy prayers
And to thy state of darkness hie thee straight:
I conjure thee by all the saints in Heaven!
   E. Ant. Peace, doting wizard, peace! I am not mad. 60
   Adr. O, that thou wert not, poor distressed soul!
   E. Ant. You minion, you, are these your customers?
Did this companion with the saffron face
Revel and feast it at my house today,
Whilst upon me the guilty doors were shut   65
And I denied to enter in my house?
   Adr. O husband, God doth know you dined at
     home;
Where would you had remained until this time,
Free from these slanders and this open shame!   70

76. **Pardie:** French *pardieu;* verily.

82. **Certes:** certainly.

96. **rag of money:** the word **rag** was slang for a farthing, a coin worth one fourth of an English penny.

E. Ant. Dined at home! Thou villain, what sayest
    thou?

E. Dro. Sir, sooth to say, you did not dine at home.

E. Ant. Were not my doors locked up and I shut
    out?   75

E. Dro. Pardie, your doors were locked and you
    shut out.

E. Ant. And did not she herself revile me there?

E. Dro. Sans fable, she herself reviled you there.

E. Ant. Did not her kitchenmaid rail, taunt, and 80
    scorn me?

E. Dro. Certes, she did; the kitchen vestal scorned
    you.

E. Ant. And did not I in rage depart from thence?

E. Dro. In verity you did; my bones bear witness, 85
That since have felt the vigor of his rage.

Adr. Is't good to soothe him in these contraries?

Pinch. It is no shame: the fellow finds his vein
And, yielding to him, humors well his frenzy.

E. Ant. Thou hast suborned the goldsmith to arrest 90
    me.

Adr. Alas, I sent you money to redeem you,
By Dromio here, who came in haste for it.

E. Dro. Money by me! Heart and good will you
    might;   95
But surely, master, not a rag of money.

E. Ant. Wentst not thou to her for a purse of
    ducats?

Adr. He came to me and I delivered it.

Luc. And I am witness with her that she did. 100

126. **make a rescue:** remove him from official custody.

E. Dro. God and the ropemaker bear me witness
That I was sent for nothing but a rope!

Pinch. Mistress, both man and master is possessed;
I know it by their pale and deadly looks.
They must be bound and laid in some dark room.   105

E. Ant. Say, wherefore didst thou lock me forth
    today?
And why dost thou deny the bag of gold?

Adr. I did not, gentle husband, lock thee forth.

E. Dro. And, gentle master, I received no gold;   110
But I confess, sir, that we were locked out.

Adr. Dissembling villain, thou speakst false in both.

E. Ant. Dissembling harlot, thou art false in all
And art confederate with a damned pack
To make a loathsome abject scorn of me: 115
But with these nails I'll pluck out these false eyes,
That would behold in me this shameful sport.

Enter three or four and offer to bind him. He strives.

Adr. O, bind him, bind him! Let him not come near
    me.

Pinch. More company! The fiend is strong within   120
    him.

Luc. Ay me, poor man, how pale and wan he looks!

E. Ant. What, will you murder me? Thou jailer,
    thou,
I am thy prisoner: wilt thou suffer them   125
To make a rescue?

130. **peevish:** foolish.

135. **discharge:** pay.

137. **grows:** arises.

141. **entered in bond:** (1) physically bound; (2) bound as a surety for his debt.

145. **cry, "The Devil":** i.e., pretend that you are possessed by a demon.

146. **idly:** madly.

Off.   Masters, let him go:
He is my prisoner, and you shall not have him.
    Pinch. Go bind this man, for he is frantic too.
                    They offer to bind Dromio of Ephesus.
    Adr. What wilt thou do, thou peevish officer?   130
Hast thou delight to see a wretched man
Do outrage and displeasure to himself?
    Off. He is my prisoner: if I let him go,
The debt he owes will be required of me.
    Adr. I will discharge thee ere I go from thee: 135
Bear me forthwith unto his creditor,
And, knowing how the debt grows, I will pay it.
Good Master Doctor, see him safe conveyed
Home to my house. O most unhappy day!
    E. Ant. O most unhappy strumpet!   140
    E. Dro. Master, I am here entered in bond for you.
    E. Ant. Out on thee, villain! wherefore dost thou
mad me?
    E. Dro. Will you be bound for nothing? Be mad,
good master: cry, "The Devil!"   145
    Luc. God help, poor souls, how idly do they talk!
    Adr. Go bear him hence. Sister, go you with me.
            Exeunt all but Adriana, Luciana, Officer and
                                Courtesan.
Say now; whose suit is he arrested at?
    Off. One Angelo, a goldsmith; do you know him?
    Adr. I know the man. What is the sum he owes?   150
    Off. Two hundred ducats.
    Adr.   Say, how grows it due?
    Off. Due for a chain your husband had of him.

161. **at large:** in full.

Adr. He did bespeak a chain for me but had it not.

Cour. Whenas your husband, all in rage, today   155
Came to my house and took away my ring—
The ring I saw upon his finger now—
Straight after did I meet him with a chain.

Adr. It may be so, but I did never see it.
Come, jailer, bring me where the goldsmith is: 160
I long to know the truth hereof at large.

*Enter Antipholus of Syracuse, with his rapier drawn,
and Dromio of Syracuse.*

Luc. God, for thy mercy! They are loose again.

Adr. And come with naked swords.
Let's call more help to have them bound again.

Off. Away! they'll kill us.   165

Exeunt omnes, as fast as may be, frighted.
[Antipholus and Dromio remain.]

S. Ant. I see these witches are afraid of swords.

S. Dro. She that would be your wife now ran from
you.

S. Ant. Come to the Centaur: fetch our stuff from
thence.   170
I long that we were safe and sound aboard.

S. Dro. Faith, stay here this night; they will surely
do us no harm. You saw they speak us fair, give us
gold. Methinks they are such a gentle nation that, but
for the mountain of mad flesh that claims marriage of   175
me, I could find in my heart to stay here still and turn
witch.

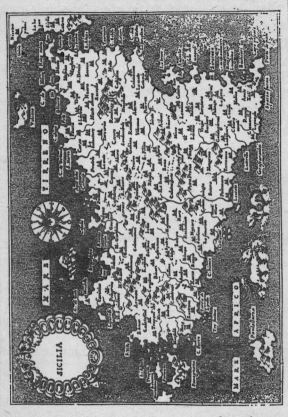

Sixteenth-century map of Sicily. Syracuse is on the southeastern coast. From Tommaso Porcacchi, *L'isole piu famose* (1590).

S. Ant. I will not stay tonight for all the town:
Therefore away, to get our stuff aboard.

                                           Exeunt.

THE COMEDY
OF ERRORS

ACT V

V. i. Antipholus of Syracuse encounters Angelo and becomes enraged at his charge that he has had a chain for which he refuses to pay. When he draws his sword, Adriana calls for help to restrain him. Antipholus and Dromio run away and take refuge in a nearby abbey. The Abbess refuses to turn over the supposed madman and rebukes Adriana for her jealousy. When the Duke appears, escorting Egeon to his execution, Adriana implores his intervention, but at this moment a messenger reports that Antipholus and Dromio have escaped and are mistreating Pinch. The second pair of twins enter shortly and Egeon recognizes Antipholus as his son. Everyone recounts his grievances at the day's confusion, but all is resolved when the Abbess comes out with the other Antipholus and Dromio and identifies herself as Egeon's long-lost wife. All are then invited to a feast to celebrate the reunion of the family.

_____

9. **His word might bear my wealth:** his credit is sufficient to command a loan equal to my whole wealth on his mere word.

11. **self:** selfsame.

ACT V

Scene I. [A street before a priory.]

*Enter [Second] Merchant and [Angelo], the
goldsmith.*

Ang. I am sorry, sir, that I have hindered you,
But, I protest, he had the chain of me,
Though most dishonestly he doth deny it.
   2nd. Mer. How is the man esteemed here in the
     city?   5
   Ang. Of very reverent reputation, sir,
Of credit infinite, highly beloved,
Second to none that lives here in the city:
His word might bear my wealth at any time.
   2nd. Mer. Speak softly: yonder, as I think, he walks.   10

*Enter Antipholus [of Syracuse] and Dromio [of
Syracuse] again.*

   Ang. 'Tis so; and that self chain about his neck
Which he forswore most monstrously to have.

17. **circumstance and oaths:** detailed protestations.

19. **charge:** expense.

36. **within him:** within his guard (a fencer's term).

Good sir, draw near to me, I'll speak to him.
Signior Antipholus, I wonder much
That you would put me to this shame and trouble;   15
And, not without some scandal to yourself,
With circumstance and oaths so to deny
This chain which now you wear so openly.
Beside the charge, the shame, imprisonment,
You have done wrong to this my honest friend,   20
Who, but for staying on our controversy,
Had hoisted sail and put to sea today.
This chain you had of me; can you deny it?

   S. Ant. I think I had. I never did deny it.

   2nd. Mer. Yes, that you did, sir, and forswore it too.   25

   S. Ant. Who heard me to deny it or forswear it?

   2nd. Mer. These ears of mine, thou knowst, did
     hear thee.
Fie on thee, wretch! 'tis pity that thou livest
To walk where any honest men resort.   30

   S. Ant. Thou art a villain to impeach me thus:
I'll prove mine honor and mine honesty
Against thee presently, if thou darest stand.

   2nd. Mer. I dare and do defy thee for a villain.
                            They draw.

Enter Adriana, Luciana, the Courtesan, and others.

   Adr. Hold, hurt him not, for God's sake! he is mad.   35
Some get within him, take his sword away.
Bind Dromio too, and bear them to my house.

38–9. **take a house:** seek refuge.
49. **heavy:** melancholy.
51. **passion:** disorder.

S. Dro. Run, master, run; for God's sake, take a
    house!
This is some priory. In, or we are spoiled!   40
    Exeunt Antipholus of Syracuse and Dromio of
                  Syracuse to the Priory.

Enter the Lady Abbess.

Abb. Be quiet, people. Wherefore throng you
    hither?
Adr. To fetch my poor distracted husband hence.
Let us come in, that we may bind him fast
And bear him home for his recovery.   45
    Ang. I knew he was not in his perfect wits.
    2nd. Mer. I am sorry now that I did draw on him.
    Abb. How long hath this possession held the man?
    Adr. This week he hath been heavy, sour, sad,
And much, much different from the man he was;   50
But till this afternoon his passion
Ne'er brake into extremity of rage.
    Abb. Hath he not lost much wealth by wrack of
    sea?
Buried some dear friend? Hath not else his eye   55
Strayed his affection in unlawful love?
A sin prevailing much in youthful men,
Who give their eyes the liberty of gazing.
Which of these sorrows is he subject to?
    Adr. To none of these, except it be the last;   60
Namely, some love that drew him oft from home.
    Abb. You should for that have reprehended him.

69. **copy:** subject; **conference:** conversation. In short, Adriana talked of nothing else.

70. **urging:** mentioning.

73. **glanced:** touched on.

74. **Still:** always; continually.

84. **sports:** pleasures.

89. **distemperatures:** ailments.

91. **or . . . or:** either . . . or.

Adr. Why, so I did.

Abb.   Ay, but not rough enough.

Adr. As roughly as my modesty would let me.   65

Abb. Haply, in private.

Adr.   And in assemblies too.

Abb. Ay, but not enough.

Adr. It was the copy of our conference:
In bed, he slept not for my urging it;   70
At board, he fed not for my urging it;
Alone, it was the subject of my theme;
In company I often glanced it;
Still did I tell him it was vile and bad.

Abb. And thereof came it that the man was mad.   75
The venom clamors of a jealous woman
Poisons more deadly than a mad dog's tooth.
It seems his sleeps were hindered by thy railing;
And thereof comes it that his head is light.
Thou sayst his meat was sauced with thy upbraidings: 80
Unquiet meals make ill digestions;
Thereof the raging fire of fever bred;
And what's a fever but a fit of madness?
Thou sayst his sports were hindered by thy brawls:
Sweet recreation barred, what doth ensue   85
But moody and dull Melancholy,
Kinsman to grim and comfortless despair;
And at her heels a huge infectious troop
Of pale distemperatures and foes to life?
In food, in sport, and life-preserving rest   90
To be disturbed would mad or man or beast:

95. **demeaned:** behaved.

97. **betray me to my own reproof:** i.e., convince me of my fault.

106. **office:** duty.

107. **attorney:** agent.

110. **approved:** proven effective by use.

112. **formal:** normal.

113. **branch . . . parcel:** synonymous: part.

117. **beseem:** befit.

The consequence is, then, thy jealous fits
Have scared thy husband from the use of wits.

  Luc. She never reprehended him but mildly,
When he demeaned himself rough, rude, and wildly. 95
Why bear you these rebukes and answer not?

  Adr. She did betray me to my own reproof.
Good people, enter, and lay hold on him.

  Abb. No, not a creature enters in my house.

  Adr. Then let your servants bring my husband forth. 100

  Abb. Neither: he took this place for sanctuary
And it shall privilege him from your hands
Till I have brought him to his wits again
Or lose my labor in assaying it.

  Adr. I will attend my husband, be his nurse, 105
Diet his sickness, for it is my office,
And will have no attorney but myself;
And therefore let me have him home with me.

  Abb. Be patient; for I will not let him stir
Till I have used the approved means I have, 110
With wholesome syrups, drugs, and holy prayers,
To make of him a formal man again:
It is a branch and parcel of mine oath,
A charitable duty of my order.
Therefore depart and leave him here with me. 115

  Adr. I will not hence and leave my husband here:
And ill it doth beseem your holiness
To separate the husband and the wife.

  Abb. Be quiet and depart: thou shalt not have him.

                                Exit.

  Luc. Complain unto the Duke of this indignity. 120

140. **tender:** offer (in mercy).

   Adr. Come, go: I will fall prostrate at his feet
And never rise until my tears and prayers
Have won His Grace to come in person hither
And take perforce my husband from the Abbess.
   2nd. Mer. By this, I think, the dial points at five: 125
Anon, I'm sure, the Duke himself in person
Comes this way to the melancholy vale,
The place of death and sorry execution,
Behind the ditches of the Abbey here.
   Ang. Upon what cause?   130
   2nd. Mer. To see a reverend Syracusian merchant,
Who put unluckily into this bay
Against the laws and statutes of this town,
Beheaded publicly for his offense.
   Ang. See where they come; we will behold his 135
     death.
   Luc. Kneel to the Duke before he pass the abbey.

*Enter Duke, attended, and Egeon bareheaded, with
     the Headsman and other Officers.*

   Duke. Yet once again proclaim it publicly,
If any friend will pay the sum for him,
He shall not die: so much we tender him. 140
   Adr. Justice, most sacred duke, against the Abbess!
   Duke. She is a virtuous and a reverend lady:
It cannot be that she hath done thee wrong.
   Adr. May it please your Grace, Antipholus my hus-
     band, 145
Who I made lord of me and all I had

147. **important:** importunate.
155. **take order for:** see to the settlement of.

At your important letters, this ill day
A most outrageous fit of madness took him;
That desp'rately he hurried through the street,
With him his bondman, all as mad as he, 150
Doing displeasure to the citizens
By rushing in their houses, bearing thence
Rings, jewels, anything his rage did like.
Once did I get him bound and sent him home,
Whilst to take order for the wrongs I went, 155
That here and there his fury had committed.
Anon, I wot not by what strong escape,
He broke from those that had the guard of him;
And with his mad attendant and himself,
Each one with ireful passion, with drawn swords, 160
Met us again, and, madly bent on us,
Chased us away; till, raising of more aid,
We came again to bind them. Then they fled
Into this abbey, whither we pursued them;
And here the Abbess shuts the gates on us 165
And will not suffer us to fetch him out
Nor send him forth, that we may bear him hence.
Therefore, most gracious Duke, with thy command
Let him be brought forth and borne hence for help.
  Duke. Long since thy husband served me in my 170
    wars;
And I to thee engaged a prince's word,
When thou didst make him master of thy bed,
To do him all the grace and good I could.
Go, some of you, knock at the Abbey gate, 175

178. shift: fly.

180. a-row: each in turn.

185. nicks him like a fool: cuts his hair jagged-ly, in such a way as to suggest the fool's coxcomb.

200. past thought of human reason: i.e., contrary to anything a human could have believed possible.

A fool with a coxcomb on his hood. From Desiderius Erasmus, *Moreas enkomion* (1676).

And bid the Lady Abbess come to me.
I will determine this before I stir.

Enter a Messenger.

Mess. O mistress, mistress, shift and save yourself!
My master and his man are both broke loose,
Beaten the maids a-row and bound the doctor,   180
Whose beard they have singed off with brands of fire;
And ever, as it blazed, they threw on him
Great pails of puddled mire to quench the hair.
My master preaches patience to him, and the while
His man with scissors nicks him like a fool;   185
And sure, unless you send some present help,
Between them they will kill the conjurer.
    Adr. Peace, fool! thy master and his man are here,
And that is false thou dost report to us.
    Mess. Mistress, upon my life, I tell you true;   190
I have not breathed almost since I did see it.
He cries for you and vows, if he can take you,
To scorch your face and to disfigure you.
                                                Cry within.
Hark, hark! I hear him, mistress: fly, be gone!
    Duke. Come, stand by me; fear nothing. Guard 195
    with halberds!
    Adr. Ay me, it is my husband! Witness you
That he is borne about invisible:
Even now we housed him in the Abbey here;
And now he's there, past thought of human reason.   200

204. **bestrid:** bestraddled his fallen body when he was wounded and fought to protect him.

213. **Even in the strength and height of injury:** to the utmost.

216. **Discover:** reveal.

219. **harlots:** not "strumpets" but "base rogues." The word **harlot** originally signified a boy of inferior position.

224. **on night:** at night.

*Enter Antipholus [of Ephesus] and Dromio of
          Ephesus.*

   E. Ant. Justice, most gracious Duke, O, grant me
    justice!
Even for the service that long since I did thee,
When I bestrid thee in the wars and took
Deep scars to save thy life; even for the blood   205
That then I lost for thee, now grant me justice.
   Ege. Unless the fear of death doth make me dote,
I see my son Antipholus and Dromio.
   E. Ant. Justice, sweet prince, against that woman
    there!   210
She whom thou gavest to me to be my wife,
That hath abused and dishonored me
Even in the strength and height of injury.
Beyond imagination is the wrong
That she this day hath shameless thrown on me.   215
   Duke. Discover how, and thou shalt find me just.
   E. Ant. This day, great Duke, she shut the doors
    upon me,
While she with harlots feasted in my house.
   Duke. A grievous fault! Say, woman, didst thou so?   220
   Adr. No, my good lord: myself, he, and my sister
Today did dine together. So befall my soul
As this is false he burdens me withal!
   Luc. Ne'er may I look on day, nor sleep on night,
But she tells to your Highness simple truth!   225

228. **am advised what I say:** speak with cool deliberation.

233. **packed:** joined in conspiracy.

253. **anatomy:** skeleton.

Ang. O perjured woman! They are both forsworn:
In this the madman justly chargeth them.
    E. Ant. My liege, I am advised what I say;
Neither disturbed with the effect of wine,
Nor heady-rash, provoked with raging ire,   230
Albeit my wrongs might make one wiser mad.
This woman locked me out this day from dinner:
That goldsmith there, were he not packed with her,
Could witness it, for he was with me then;
Who parted with me to go fetch a chain,   235
Promising to bring it to the Porpentine,
Where Balthazar and I did dine together.
Our dinner done, and he not coming thither,
I went to seek him: in the street I met him,
And in his company that gentleman.   240
There did this perjured goldsmith swear me down
That I this day of him received the chain,
Which, God He knows, I saw not: for the which
He did arrest me with an officer.
I did obey and sent my peasant home   245
For certain ducats; he with none returned.
Then fairly I bespoke the officer
To go in person with me to my house.
By the way we met my wife, her sister, and a rabble
        more   250
Of vile confederates. Along with them
They brought one Pinch, a hungry, lean-faced villain,
A mere anatomy, a mountebank,
A threadbare juggler and a fortuneteller,
A needy, hollow-eyed, sharp-looking wretch,   255

257. **Forsooth:** indeed; **took on him as:** pretended to be; **conjurer:** exorcist.

A living dead man. This pernicious slave,
Forsooth, took on him as a conjurer,
And, gazing in mine eyes, feeling my pulse,
And with no face, as 'twere, outfacing me,
Cries out I was possessed. Then all together   260
They fell upon me, bound me, bore me thence,
And in a dark and dankish vault at home
There left me and my man, both bound together;
Till, gnawing with my teeth my bonds in sunder,
I gained my freedom and immediately   265
Ran hither to your Grace, whom I beseech
To give me ample satisfaction
For these deep shames and great indignities.
    Ang. My lord, in truth, thus far I witness with him,
That he dined not at home but was locked out.   270
    Duke. But had he such a chain of thee or no?
    Ang. He had, my lord; and when he ran in here,
These people saw the chain about his neck.
    2nd. Mer. Besides, I will be sworn these ears of
        mine   275
Heard you confess you had the chain of him,
After you first forswore it on the mart,
And thereupon I drew my sword on you.
And then you fled into this abbey here,
From whence, I think, you are come by miracle.   280
    E. Ant. I never came within these Abbey walls;
Nor ever didst thou draw thy sword on me:
I never saw the chain, so help me Heaven!
And this is false you burden me withal.
    Duke. Why, what an intricate impeach is this!   285

286. **Circe's cup:** the potion by which the witch Circe of Homer's *Odyssey* transformed men into beasts.

300. **mated:** confounded.

303. **Haply:** perhaps.

Circe with some of her victims. From Geoffrey Whitney, *A Choice of Emblems* (1586).

I think you all have drunk of Circe's cup.
If here you housed him, here he would have been;
If he were mad, he would not plead so coldly.
You say he dined at home; the goldsmith here
Denies that saying. Sirrah, what say you?   290

  E. Dro. Sir, he dined with her there, at the Porpentine.

  Cour. He did; and from my finger snatched that ring.

  E. Ant. 'Tis true, my liege, this ring I had of her. 295

  Duke. Sawst thou him enter at the Abbey here?

  Cour. As sure, my liege, as I do see your Grace.

  Duke. Why, this is strange. Go call the Abbess hither.

I think you are all mated, or stark mad.   300

                    Exit one to the Abbess.

  Ege. Most mighty Duke, vouchsafe me speak a word:

Haply I see a friend will save my life
And pay the sum that may deliver me.

  Duke. Speak freely, Syracusian, what thou wilt.   305

  Ege. Is not your name, sir, called Antipholus?
And is not that your bondman, Dromio?

  E. Dro. Within this hour I was his bondman, sir,
But he, I thank him, gnawed in two my cords:
Now am I Dromio and his man unbound.   310

  Ege. I am sure you both of you remember me.

  E. Dro. Ourselves we do remember, sir, by you;
For lately we were bound, as you are now.
You are not Pinch's patient, are you, sir?

320. **careful:** full of care (grief).
321. **defeatures:** disfigurements.
333. **grained:** lined.
338. **to hear:** i.e., of hearing.

Ege. Why look you strange on me? You know me 315
well.

E. Ant. I never saw you in my life till now.

Ege. O, grief hath changed me since you saw me
last,

And careful hours with time's deformed hand 320
Have written strange defeatures in my face:
But tell me yet, dost thou not know my voice?

E. Ant. Neither.

Ege. Dromio, nor thou?

E. Dro. No, trust me, sir, nor I. 325

Ege. I am sure thou dost.

E. Dro. Ay, sir, but I am sure I do not; and whatso-
ever a man denies, you are now bound to believe him.

Ege. Not know my voice! O time's extremity,
Hast thou so cracked and splitted my poor tongue 330
In seven short years that here my only son
Knows not my feeble key of untuned cares?
Though now this grained face of mine be hid
In sap-consuming winter's drizzled snow,
And all the conduits of my blood froze up, 335
Yet hath my night of life some memory,
My wasting lamps some fading glimmer left,
My dull deaf ears a little use to hear.
All these old witnesses—I cannot err—
Tell me thou art my son Antipholus. 340

E. Ant. I never saw my father in my life.

Ege. But seven years since, in Syracusa, boy,
Thou knowst we parted: but perhaps, my son,
Thou shamest to acknowledge me in misery.

355. **genius:** guardian spirit.

E. Ant. The Duke and all that know me in the city 345
Can witness with me that it is not so:
I ne'er saw Syracusa in my life.

Duke. I tell thee, Syracusian, twenty years
Have I been patron to Antipholus,
During which time he ne'er saw Syracusa: 350
I see thy age and dangers make thee dote.

*Enter the Abbess, with Antipholus of Syracuse and
Dromio of Syracuse.*

Abb. Most mighty Duke, behold a man much
     wronged.   *All gather to see them.*
Adr. I see two husbands, or mine eyes deceive me.
Duke. One of these men is genius to the other; 355
And so of these. Which is the natural man,
And which the spirit? Who deciphers them?
S. Dro. I, sir, am Dromio; command him away.
E. Dro. I, sir, am Dromio; pray, let me stay.
S. Ant. Egeon art thou not? or else his ghost? 360
S. Dro. O, my old master! Who hath bound him
     here?
Abb. Whoever bound him, I will loose his bonds
And gain a husband by his liberty.
Speak, old Egeon, if thou beest the man 365
That hadst a wife once called Emilia,
That bore thee at a burden two fair sons.
O, if thou beest the same Egeon, speak,
And speak unto the same Emilia!

374. **urging:** mention. Apparently a slip on Shakespeare's part, since the Abbess has not mentioned the shipwreck.

Duke [*Aside*] Why, here begins his morning story 370
   right:
These two Antipholus', these two so like,
And these two Dromios, one in semblance—
Besides her urging of her wrack at sea—
These are the parents to these children,   375
Which accidentally are met together.
  Ege. If I dream not, thou art Emilia:
If thou art she, tell me, where is that son
That floated with thee on the fatal raft?
  Abb. By men of Epidamnum he and I   380
And the twin Dromio all were taken up;
But by and by rude fishermen of Corinth
By force took Dromio and my son from them,
And me they left with those of Epidamnum.
What then became of them I cannot tell: 385
I to this fortune that you see me in.
  Duke. Antipholus, thou camest from Corinth first?
  S. Ant. No, sir, not I; I came from Syracuse.
  Duke. Stay, stand apart; I know not which is which.
  E. Ant. I came from Corinth, my most gracious 390
   lord—
  E. Dro. And I with him.
  E. Ant. Brought to this town by that most famous
   warrior,
Duke Menaphon, your most renowned uncle.   395
  Adr. Which of you two did dine with me today?
  S. Ant. I, gentle mistress.
  Adr.   And are not you my husband?
  E. Ant. No, I say nay to that.

404. **make good:** prove
415. **still:** always.
427. **sympathized:** mutually experienced.

S. *Ant.* And so do I; yet did she call me so: 400
And this fair gentlewoman, her sister here,
Did call me brother. [*To Luciana*] What I told you
    then
I hope I shall have leisure to make good,
If this be not a dream I see and hear.   405
    Ang. That is the chain, sir, which you had of me.
    S. *Ant.* I think it be, sir; I deny it not.
    E. *Ant.* And you, sir, for this chain arrested me.
    Ang. I think I did, sir: I deny it not.
    Adr. I sent you money, sir, to be your bail,   410
By Dromio; but I think he brought it not.
    E. *Dro.* No, none by me.
    S. *Ant.* This purse of ducats I received from you,
And Dromio my man did bring them me.
I see we still did meet each other's man;   415
And I was ta'en for him and he for me;
And thereupon these errors are arose.
    E. *Ant.* These ducats pawn I for my father here.
    Duke. It shall not need; thy father hath his life.
    Cour. Sir, I must have that diamond from you.   420
    E. *Ant.* There, take it, and much thanks for my
        good cheer.
    Abb. Renowned Duke, vouchsafe to take the pains
To go with us into the Abbey here
And hear at large discoursed all our fortunes: 425
And all that are assembled in this place,
That by this sympathized one day's error
Have suffered wrong, go keep us company,
And we shall make full satisfaction.

430. **Thirty-three years:** apparently a mistake. Other indications of the lapse of time would make the twins twenty-five years of age. See I. i. 126 and line 331 of this scene.

434. **calendars:** reminders of time.

435. **gossips' feast:** christening feast. **Gossip** originally meant "godparent."

442. **lay at host:** were checked at the inn.

448. **kitchened:** entertained in the kitchen.

450. **glass:** mirror.

Elizabethan christening. From Richard Day, *A Book of Christian Prayers* (1590).

Thirty-three years have I but gone in travail   430
Of you, my sons, and till this present hour
My heavy burden ne'er delivered.
The Duke, my husband, and my children both,
And you the calendars of their nativity,
Go to a gossips' feast, and go with me;   435
After so long grief, such nativity!
    Duke. With all my heart, I'll gossip at this feast.
            Exeunt [all but Antipholus of Syracuse,
            Antipholus of Ephesus, Dromio of
            Syracuse, and Dromio of Ephesus].
    S. Dro. Master, shall I fetch your stuff from ship-
    board?
    E. Ant. Dromio, what stuff of mine hast thou em- 440
    barked?
    S. Dro. Your goods that lay at host, sir, in the
    Centaur.
    S. Ant. He speaks to me. I am your master, Dromio.
Come, go with us; we'll look to that anon.   445
Embrace thy brother there; rejoice with him.
    Exeunt [Antipholus of Syracuse and Antipholus of
                  Ephesus].
    S. Dro. There is a fat friend at your master's house
That kitchened me for you today at dinner:
She now shall be my sister, not my wife.
    E. Dro. Methinks you are my glass and not my 450
    brother:
I see by you I am a sweet-faced youth.
Will you walk in to see their gossiping?
    S. Dro. Not I, sir: you are my elder.

455. **try:** determine.

456. **cuts:** lots (by lengths of straw or other material).

Thirty-three years have I but gone in travail   430
Of you, my sons, and till this present hour
My heavy burden ne'er delivered.
The Duke, my husband, and my children both,
And you the calendars of their nativity,
Go to a gossips' feast, and go with me;   435
After so long grief, such nativity!
    Duke. With all my heart, I'll gossip at this feast.
                    Exeunt [all but Antipholus of Syracuse,
                        Antipholus of Ephesus, Dromio of
                            Syracuse, and Dromio of Ephesus].
    S. Dro. Master, shall I fetch your stuff from ship-
        board?
    E. Ant. Dromio, what stuff of mine hast thou em- 440
        barked?
    S. Dro. Your goods that lay at host, sir, in the
        Centaur.
    S. Ant. He speaks to me. I am your master, Dromio.
Come, go with us; we'll look to that anon.   445
Embrace thy brother there; rejoice with him.
    Exeunt [Antipholus of Syracuse and Antipholus of
                                    Ephesus].
    S. Dro. There is a fat friend at your master's house
That kitchened me for you today at dinner:
She now shall be my sister, not my wife.
    E. Dro. Methinks you are my glass and not my   450
        brother:
I see by you I am a sweet-faced youth.
Will you walk in to see their gossiping?
    S. Dro. Not I, sir: you are my elder.

455. **try:** determine.

456. **cuts:** lots (by lengths of straw or other material).

E. Dro. That's a question; how shall we try it?   455

S. Dro. We'll draw cuts for the senior; till then lead
  thou first.

E. Dro. Nay, then, thus:
We came into the world like brother and brother;
And now let's go hand in hand, not one before an-   460
  other.

                              Exeunt.

KEY TO
Famous Lines

The pleasing punishment that women bear.   [*Egeon*—I. i. 47]

We may pity though not pardon thee.   [*Duke*—I. i. 98]

To tell sad stories of my own mishaps.   [*Egeon*—I. i. 121]

Headstrong liberty is lashed with woe.   [*Luciana*—II. i. 15]

They say every why hath a wherefore. [*S. Dromio*—II. ii. 47-8]

What he hath scanted men in hair, he hath
  given them in wit.   [*S. Dromio*—II. ii. 87-8]

Small cheer and great welcome makes a merry feast.
                [*Balthazar*—III. i. 36-7]

There is something in the wind.   [*E. Antipholus*—III. i. 117]

We'll pluck a crow together.   [*E. Dromio*—III. i. 144-45]

The venom clamors of a jealous woman
Poisons more deadly than a mad dog's tooth.
                [*Abbess*—V. i. 76-7]